THE BURNING

Parenting my son through adoption, FASD, and suicide

Ruth Spencer

Title: The Burning: Parenting my son through adoption, FASD, and suicide.
Author: Ruth Spencer
Published by A.F.S.BOOKS

Copyright © 2019 by A.F.S.BOOKS
All rights reserved. No portion of this book, except for brief review, may be reproduced, stored in a retrieval system, or transmitted in any form or by any means without written permission of the author.

Cover Design: James Spencer and Tim Spencer
Book Design: Jim Bisakowski bookdesign.ca
Editors: Sara Graefe, Rachel J. Peterson, and Page Two.
Author contact: P.O. Box 21088, Duncan B.C. V9L 3P8

ISBN: 978-0-9948892-0-1 (e-book)
ISBN: 978-0-9948892-2-5 (book

> Library and Archives Canada Cataloguing in Publication
>
> Title: The burning : parenting my son through adoption, FASD, and suicide / Ruth Spencer.
> Names: Spencer, Ruth, 1946- author.
> Identifiers: Canadiana (print) 20190112689 | Canadiana (ebook) 20190112697 | ISBN 9780994889218
>   (softcover) | ISBN 9780994889201 (PDF)
> Subjects: LCSH: Spencer, Ruth, 1946- | LCSH: Spencer, Ruth, 1946- —Family. | LCSH: Spencer, Alex,
>   1976-2002. | LCSH: Adoptive parents—Canada—Biography. | LCSH: Mothers of suicide victims—Canada—
>   Biography. | LCSH: Parents of children with disabilities—Canada—Biography. | LCSH: Adopted
>   children—Canada—Biography. | LCSH: Suicide victims—Canada—Biography. | LCSH: Fetal alcohol
>   spectrum disorders—Patients—Canada—Biography. | LCSH: Adoption—Canada. | LCGFT: Autobiographies.
> Classification: LCC HV874.82.S64 A3 2019 | DDC 362.734092—dc23

This book is a memoir. It presents the author's present recollections of past experiences. Some names have been changed, some dialogue has been modified, and some characters have been made more sympathetic.

Printed in Canada

Elizabeth Mary Clare Marten 1943—2003

*For my dear friend Clare, who,
even though she did not always understand,
always loved.*

Contents

Extinguished. .9
Writing an Obituary 15
1999. 24
Passing the Torch 33
Mary Grace 39
The Coroner's Visit 50
An Underground Spark. 67
The Chapel. 73
The Sparks Begin to Fly. 80
Fanning the Flames. 87
Psych Ward. 96
Smouldering. 112
Memories. 123
Finding Positives in the Negatives. 133
Clothes for the Burning. 141
Planning the Funeral 146
Flickering Coals 151
Alex's Last Flame 162
Back Burning 171
Another Little Bonfire 177
Beacon of Hope 190
The Funeral 199
The Reception 210
The Burning 218
Appendix i 224
Appendix ii. 227
Appendix iii 230
About the Author 233
Book Club Material 234

Acknowledgements

Thank you to my readers—Gail, Myra, Elli, Griti, Jamie, Marjorie, Linda, Marilyn, Eileen, Jack, Diana, Jen, Cathy, Vera and Hans, Dave, and Winnie.

Some of you read for content and continuity,
some of you eliminated adverbs,
some of you checked legalities and adoption details,
some of you knew more than most about FASD and suicide,
some of you noted confusing Canadian idioms,
and all of you have waited for ten years to finally see this page.

Extinguished

The telephone was ringing.

I roused from a deep sleep, opened one eye, and saw nothing but midnight darkness. Peter was still asleep but not for long; I poked at his shoulder. "Peter? Are you awake? It's the phone."

He grunted and rolled over as the noise stopped and the answering machine clicked on. Snuggling down in my warm cozy bed, I wondered sleepily who could be calling us in the middle of the night.

The phone rang again. Outside, our three dogs were barking.

"Somebody wants us. Maybe it's an emergency," said Peter, abruptly wide-awake. "I'll go out and see what's the matter with the dogs; they're going to wake the whole neighbourhood." That left the phone for me to deal with.

We both sat up. Peter turned on his bedside lamp while I reached for my housecoat, grumbling, "By the time I get up to the kitchen, that answering machine will have got it,"…but the caller didn't leave a message. When the phone began ringing for the third time, I had already arrived at the top of the basement stairs. Hustling across the kitchen and snatching up the receiver, I snapped, "Hello!"

"This is Constable Gustafsson, RCMP," said a woman's voice.

The police. We were used to hearing from them, although not in the middle of the night. What had Tim, our family's black sheep, done this time? In the silent second that followed, I felt my stomach tense and my face whiten.

"Is this Ruth Spencer?"

"Yes."

"I'm parked in your driveway, but your dogs won't let me get out of my vehicle."

"My husband is bringing the dogs inside," I told her. Needing to know the worst first, I caught hold of a kitchen chair for support and asked sharply, "Why are you here?"

"I've come to talk to you about your son Alexander," said Constable Gustafsson. So, this wasn't about Tim.

The next thing that flashed through my mind was *traffic accident* and my heart dropped into my slippers. Our second son, Zan, officially Alexander David, was a good driver who enjoyed speed; he now lived in Victoria. Our fourth son, Alexander Bellman, who was usually called Alex, lived here in town, but he didn't own a car.

"I have two sons named Alexander. Is it the tall blond one or the short dark one?"

"Dark," said Constable Gustafsson tersely. Alex, I thought with relief. Of all my four sons, he was the one least likely to be out driving a car at night and the one most likely to need Mom to sort something out.

The dogs weren't barking anymore, so I knew Peter had everything under control outside. "I'll meet you at the front door," I said. Glancing at the clock, for the first time that morning, I added in surprise, "Do you know what time it is?"

"I'm well aware of the time, ma'am," she replied shortly.

Needing, as always, to smooth away confrontation, I said, "Golly, I wasn't." It was nearly 3 a.m.

Having dealt with the dogs, Peter now stood in the hallway at the top of the basement stairs, pulling on his bathrobe and looking apprehensive. Moving past him to open the front door, I said, "It's something about Alex."

Thanks to our Tim's escapades, I was used to greeting the police at my door. They were usually male, heavy set and going bald. Constable Gustafsson looked, at least to me, much too young and slight to be a police officer. She was a redhead, about my height, with watchful eyes. She refused the coffee Peter offered to make and suggested we all sit down. Peter led the way to the dining room where we settled around the table.

"Mr. Spencer, Mrs. Spencer," the Constable got right into it, "I'm sorry to have to tell you this. Your son, Alexander, committed suicide tonight." Her words seemed to hang in the air.

I waited for her to say the next bit…that my son would soon be okay…that somebody was already looking into correcting this difficulty…that everything would be fine…but she didn't say anything. Neither did Peter.

Eventually, I broke the silence. "Do you mean he's dead?"

She nodded. "Yes."

And suddenly it was true—a flat, stolid, inflexible reality. I knew completely and irrevocably that our lives, Alex's and mine, had been snapped apart. Alex was gone—forever.

Behind that knowledge there was nothing. My mind had already slipped into its level, emotion blocking mode. This almost automatic response to any emotional strain had started with a severe traumatic stress disorder nine years earlier. Although I didn't know it yet, my feelings were shutting down.

I said, almost casually, "Well, I always knew he wouldn't make old bones."

"You don't seem surprised."

"I am." Peter's voice cracked, and his hand, resting on the table, trembled slightly.

"I'm not," I said. "I'm shocked, but I'm not surprised."

For the last seven years, ever since he was eighteen, Alex had been seeking attention with staged suicide attempts. He had not come anywhere near death because dying wasn't ever part of his plan. What he truly wanted, and always hoped for, was admission to the hospital psychiatric ward, one of his favourite places.

Long ago, our family doctor had offered a frightening warning. "You had better prepare yourself," he told me, "because one of these bogus attempts might succeed. Alex is playing an extremely dangerous game."

"Are you allowed to tell us what happened?" Peter asked.

"Of course. That's why I'm here," said Constable Gustafsson.

One of the tenants in Alex's building, who lived in apartment 205, had called the manager at 11p.m. with a complaint. Loud music had been coming from 305, directly above him, for the last two hours. He had tried to phone that apartment several times, but nobody answered.

The building manager asked a woman who lived on the third floor, across the hall in 306, to witness his opening of Alex's door with a passkey. They found Alex lying on the bathroom floor. He had been dead for about two hours.

"It was definitely a suicide," Constable Gustafsson told us. "Your son hung himself using the shower curtain rod. No foul play is suspected."

She opened a black daybook and checked her notes. "The coroner has already been to Alex's apartment, and she will want to talk to you. She'll be phoning later today."

I was handed a card with 'Sherry Foster, Coroner' written across it.

"The body has been taken to the hospital morgue."

The body. This was my Alex, my precious youngest we were discussing. This wasn't 'the body.' Still, I found Constable Gustafsson's efficient professionalism and her lack of sentiment bracing rather than upsetting.

"You can make arrangements with the hospital if you want to see him." She checked her notes again. "The body has already been identified by a member of the family."

I swiftly catalogued our family members. Who would have been anywhere near Alex's apartment at that time of night? And surely whoever had been trusted to identify him would have called us before now?

Again, Peter put the question, "Which one?"

"Your son's cousin. She had arranged to visit him at 9 p.m., but she didn't get there until 11:30 p.m."

Alex had two cousins living here in Alderlea, but it seemed unlikely either of them would be visiting him at nearly midnight.

"One of my brother's girls?" I asked.

"She's an older woman. First Nations."

"Oh, right," I remembered. "Alex told me she was coming to visit him on Wednesday night. He didn't know her." I directed my explanation towards Peter, who was sitting beside me. "Alex said he was walking in town last week when somebody drove past and yelled, 'Are you Bellman? I'm your cousin.' He didn't catch her name, but while the light was red, he gave her his phone number and address."

Constable Gustafsson raised her eyebrows. "He gave his address to a stranger?"

"Typical Alex," was Peter's comment.

"Yes, but Alex doesn't understand about strangers," I reminded him and added, for the constable's benefit, "He thinks anyone who pays attention to him is his best friend."

I turned back to Constable Gustafsson and asked, "Have you talked to anybody else in our family? Does Tim know about this?" As well as being brothers, Tim and Alex were good friends.

For the first time, the officer seemed a little flustered.

"I haven't told Tim," she said. "His name was in your son's wallet as next of kin but your name was there too, so I came here." She closed her daybook, and added, "Tim and I have had trouble in the past during some of his arrests and incarcerations. I didn't think it would do him any good to get this kind of news from me."

I nodded, understanding her desire to avoid making a bad situation worse. Tim, our third son, was a regular client of the legal system and corrections. For the last nine years he had been either in jail or on probation. His attitude toward the local police was, at best, belligerent.

"Actually," I said, "Tim is doing pretty well these days; his girlfriend sees to that. But they moved recently, so probably the address in Alex's wallet isn't right."

In the pause that followed, Peter wiped away a tear and reached toward me. I gave his hand a comforting squeeze.

Constable Gustafsson asked, "Is there anybody you folks could call now?"

"Not at this time of night," said Peter. "We'll phone the family in the morning."

I was longing to connect with Mary Grace, who had been my

counsellor, support and safety net for nine years, ever since Tim's first arrest. But I agreed with Peter, 3:30 a.m. was not an appropriate time to disturb somebody who had to be at work in a few hours. Mary Grace was the Pastoral Care Coordinator at the hospital; I could call her there at 9 a.m.

Constable Gustafsson stayed another half hour, giving Peter and me time to ask more questions. She told us Generations, one of the local funeral services, had already sent a vehicle to take Alex from his apartment to the hospital morgue. She explained the coroner's role and assured us that a coroner was always called if a death was unexpected. She gave me her office phone number, and her shifts for the next few days in case we needed to be in touch.

When she was ready to go, I said, "Thank you for staying so long. This must have been a very hard night for you."

We hugged each other. Appreciating my sympathy, she fleetingly became just another woman, sobbing softly into my shoulder. Within seconds, though, she was again an official police officer, upright and ready for action.

"Try to get some sleep," she said briskly as she left.

Writing an Obituary

Sleep was the farthest thing from our minds; we both wanted to be busy. Peter made coffee, whistling sharply throughout the process, while I wandered around the dark house, concentrating on all the extra work and organization that would need to be done over the next few days. When the coffee was ready we took our mugs back to the dining room table. Peter hid himself behind yesterday's paper while I tried to write an obituary for Alex.

My first complication was his date of birth. The social worker who brought little Alex to our house, twenty-three years before, told me, "His birthday is October 25," and that became our celebration date. But a few days later, when I called to make an appointment with his out-of-town doctor, the receptionist said, "That's October 18, 1976, right?" Alex's previous hospital records had him listed as an October 27 birth; Health and Welfare Canada, the only federal department we had to deal with, knew the correct date was October 31. For the obit, I decided to use the date on his birth certificate, sent to us by the provincial government when his adoption was completed.

That led to another question. Was it necessary to put down 'adopted son of Peter and Ruth Spencer?' Many obituaries clarified relationships by including the status of 'foster,' 'step,' or 'adopted,' but did it matter if Alex was adopted or genetically linked? He was our son and we loved him—that's what counted. I thought back to the many strangers and new acquaintances who had asked, right in front of the children, "And which ones are *really* yours?" Sometimes, when our numbers rose to seven or eight, or if we had two babies who were clearly not twins, this was a legitimate question but, in my opinion, a discourteous one. A crisp "All of them," was my standard answer.

Should any of our forty odd children be named in the obit? Some had stayed for a few weeks or a few months, but others had been with us for a year or even longer. Some, now adults, had kept in touch for many years; others had vanished from our lives although not from our photograph albums. Over a seventeen-year span, we had been blessed with foster children, foreign exchange students, the progeny of friends and relations, unaccompanied minors from Vietnam, child boarders, and babies waiting for adoption. But privacy laws prevented foster children from being listed; I resolved to disregard all the extras and include siblings only. Alex had four of those, all older than himself. Kathleen was our adopted oldest, our first child and also our first foster child; she came to us at nearly three, unable to walk or talk and weighing only fifteen pounds. James, four years younger than Kathleen, and Zan, three years younger than James, were our birth sons. Timmy, our first adopted son, joined the family as a foster child when he was eighteen months old. He and Zanny, also eighteen months, clicked together and clung like two little magnets. Alex was a year younger than my 'twins' and, like Tim and Kathleen, of First Nations descent.

The next paragraph of the obit should have been less complicated – an overview of Alex's life and general interests – but as I wrote 'Lomas Elementary School' memories of the many services he had desperately needed but never received moved to the front of my thinking.

As a small child, Alex had a hard time putting his words together correctly and in the right order. Phrases that had been cute when he was three—("unsidey bout" for "inside out" and "awe va lit" for "all of it")—and were still faintly amusing at four—("look him did" for "look at what he did" and "not her coming" for "she isn't coming")—became worrying by the time he turned five. When Alex started grade one, I asked about speech therapy because he continued to say, "us am going?" for "are we going?" and "us gots it" for "we have it," and the other children in his classroom were beginning to notice.

"Speech therapy wouldn't help him," I was told. "Well, what else have you got?" I asked. "He needs *something*." But the school had nothing. To fill the void, we began an intensive home therapy program that involved the whole family.

Peter and I encouraged Alex to listen more carefully and had him constantly repeat—first single words, then phrases, and finally whole sentences. Kathleen and James read his library books to him over and over again. I kept the peace during breakfast and lunch on weekdays by reading more advanced books aloud for everybody. The grade three classes formed a speech choir; Tim and Zan practiced loudly and often. Grandma, a splendid storyteller, repeated the tales that had fascinated my brother and I when we were small. Alex was inundated with words.

Soon we were noticing changes in his pronunciation, then in his word use and finally in his sentence structure. When it was time for class photos for all, and individual photos for those who could afford them, Alex, who couldn't get hold of the word 'individual,' said, "It's the class picture what you stand by yourself." And the following spring, when James was determined to wear shorts to school (nobody wore shorts to school during the early eighties) I asked the others, "Doesn't everybody in your room wear long pants?"

"No," said Alex. "Some of them was wearing his dress."

Throughout his elementary school years, Alex was classed as a slow learner. He managed to maintain low average marks in most subjects, but arithmetic was a real challenge and he was hopeless when it came to telling time. He and Daddy worked with a toy clock, and Alex learned the hours, but the minutes were a concept he couldn't grasp. Digital time, and a new watch for his tenth birthday, saved him. He could then say with confidence, "five seventeen" or "eight forty three" and nobody except family knew that he still didn't understand what the numbers meant.

Velcro was not yet in common use in the early 80s. Peter took on the task of teaching Alex to tie his own shoelaces. It was another major struggle, partly because of Alex's poor hand-eye coordination, and partly because dangling laces didn't worry him. But one day he discovered a good reason to keep his laces done up. It was a day none of us would forget.

We had spent the morning at the Royal Museum in Victoria. By noon we were all hungry and ready for a picnic in Beacon Hill Park. Peter said, "Lunch time!" and the kids ran ahead, eager to go down on the crowded escalator. They were still young enough to find this an exciting ride. Peter and I were several stairs behind because a group of elderly ladies had stepped on between parents and children.

James reached the bottom and jumped off, with Tim and Zan right behind him. Kathleen was a little more careful. Next, it was Alex's turn, but Alex was stuck. His shoelace, undone as usual, had caught inside the rolling step, and he was quickly pulled to his knees. Peter and I, halfway down, could only watch in horror as the group of elderly ladies started to pile up against Alex. James ran back to support his brother, and two guards sprang forward and started hauling the ladies off the moving stairs and swinging them beyond the rails on either side. Peter grabbed my arm and pulled me backwards, trying to give the guards a bit more space to manoeuvre. In seconds, the last few stairs were free of people. Peter and I stepped off as the older guard lifted Alex and stood him on his feet. The other guard started to yell at him.

"You get those shoelaces tied up, and don't ever let me see them like that again!" Alex squatted and got to work with shaking hands. The other kids, gathering round, received their share of the scolding. "You're all bigger than him—you should have made sure he was safe! Now, all of you, before you ever step onto another escalator, you check your shoelaces! Is that clear?"

They nodded, muttered apologies, and started toward the door, a very subdued little group. Peter and I stopped to thank the guards for both the quick rescue and the splendid lecture. We were so glad we didn't have to deliver it ourselves.

Middle school and high school were easier for Alex than

elementary school had been. There were special classes in core subjects for the slower learners. Being, by then, an experienced parent who knew the system, I had him removed from compulsory French during his first week at Dwyer Middle School, insisting on extra help for maths instead. Alex liked his co-ed sewing and cooking classes, endured art and choir, hid in the washrooms when it was time for P.E., and thoroughly enjoyed being in the trumpet section of the band. He had a lot of musical help because Zan also played trumpet (and later baritone horn) in the same middle school and high school bands. In those few years, we were a melodious family. The boys were members of the Prevost Valley Air Cadet band, with Zan and Alex playing their trumpets, and Tim and James enjoying both drums and glockenspiel. Kathleen was learning guitar. Peter played guitar, accordion, and an old pump organ. They all practiced at home. Ours was not a quiet household.

I wanted to mention Scouts Canada in Alex's obit. From Beavers and Brownies through to Pathfinders and Venturers, our whole family had been immersed in the Canadian Guiding and Scouting Movements. Alex, along with his brothers, was a Beaver, then a Five Star Cub, and later a Scout. The three younger boys had finished as Police Venturers. In his last two years of high school, James became a Beaver leader. About the same time, Kathleen, now too old for Pathfinders, started helping with the local Cub pack. I had been a member of several Group Committees; Peter had been a parent driver. It was good for Alex, with his many learning disabilities (the elementary school principal said, "Alex has learning disabilities that haven't been discovered yet") to be part of a structured, well-supervised, noncompetitive service group where he could be successful.

I didn't want to say anything about his adult employment record, which, thanks to those same learning disabilities, was distinctly *un*successful. Some of Alex's deficits, chief among them his poor ability to balance, had shown up very early. Others, including his low IQ, lack of impulse control, intermittent memory, and missing reasoning ability, were revealed as he grew older. When he was thirteen, Alex was referred to Sunny Hill Children's Hospital in Vancouver for Fetal Alcohol Spectrum Disorder (FASD) testing. He was diagnosed with full Fetal Alcohol Syndrome. As an adult, his smart appearance, excellent vocabulary, and eager attitude promised employers far more than he could deliver. Until he started working for the FASD community, all his jobs were short term, and he never seemed to know why he had been fired.

Alex wasn't our only alcohol affected child. Kathleen and Tim had also been exposed to alcohol before birth and were born with Fetal Alcohol Spectrum Disorders. Kathleen, although she struggled through school as a slow learner, had a practical mind and a fair share of life skills. She was a grade twelve graduate; she could manage both time and money well; she was able to make and keep appointments; her driving record was unblemished. And so, when expensive FASD testing for adults finally became available, we were surprised to learn that her primary diagnosis was mild mental handicap. ARND (Alcohol Related Neurodevelopmental Disorder) was her secondary diagnosis.

But Tim, athletic, attractive, intelligent, and popular, was the most unlucky member of the family. His invisible disabilities led him into constant trouble with the law. Tim had been tested at Sunny Hill through Juvenile Forensics eight years before, soon after his eighteenth birthday. His diagnosis of FAE (Fetal Alcohol Effect) didn't change a thing. Tim was still being punished for—rather than being helped because of—his brain damage.

In spite of having three adult children with special needs, Peter and I knew we were among the fortunate because, years before, anxious parents of children with Fetal Alcohol Spectrum Disorders had found each other and had formed a support group. Belonging to that group saved us all from despair. In 1998, we officially became the Prevost Valley FASD Action Team Society. Now, as we continued to parent permanent teenagers, we all worked hard to make our town FASD friendly. We educated anybody who would listen and did all we could to change the future for children born, like ours, with permanent brain damage.

Our society opened a small storefront headquarters, one of the first in Canada. We employed Alex and several other young adults with FASD as part of a mentorship team working out of our office. The team mentored those who either had an official diagnosis or who thought they might have FASD. These young folk and their supporters were the people who best understood Alex's gifts and deficits, his open heart and caring attitude, his active attention seeking and poor judgment. I knew they would be devastated.

Pulling it all together, I drafted a short obituary:

> Alexander Bellman Spencer:
> October 20, 1976 – May 20, 2002
>
> Lovingly remembered by his father and mother, Peter and Ruth Spencer, his brothers James (Elaine), Timothy (Suzanne), and Alexander David, and his sister, Kathleen (Joseph). Will be sadly missed by his little daughter, Kaitlyn, and her mother, Cricket.
>
> Alex spent most of his life in Alderlea. He attended Lomas Elementary School and was active in First Prevost Valley Beavers and Cubs, Second Alderlea Scouts, and First Alderlea Police Venturers. A member of the Royal Canadian Air Cadets, he played trumpet in the air cadet band and his two school bands, Dwyer Middle School and Prevost Valley Senior Secondary.
>
> He was a lifelong member of St. Cecelia's Roman Catholic Church.
>
> Alex was involved with the Mentorship Team of Finding Alternative Solutions and served on the Board of Directors of the Prevost Valley FASD Action Team Society as assistant secretary. He spoke publicly about Fetal Alcohol Spectrum Disorder on many occasions to help educate his community regarding the complications of living with an invisible disability.
>
> Donations in memory of Alex can be made to the Prevost Valley FASD Action Team Society.

"Well, that's done, except for a funeral date and time," I said, throwing down my pencil, "And it's exactly like every other obit. Doesn't say a thing about the real Alex."

Peter put aside his paper. He was remarkably calm for a man who usually lost his temper at the first sign of family crisis. "Do you want to read it to me?" he asked. Reading aloud was my favourite way of checking the flow of a piece, and Peter was my best listener.

"No, it's fine for now," I said. "We need to decide who we're going to phone, and everything else we'll have to do. I think this will be a long morning."

We began a list of family and friends who cared about Alex and would want to share this new burden, starting with Cricket, one of Alex's ex-girlfriends and the mother of our only grandchild, Kaitlyn, Alex's three year old daughter. They lived in Alberta, where the time was an hour ahead of ours. Cricket could be called at 6:30 a.m. It was her right to be the first to know.

Next on the list were Alex's four siblings. Kathleen lived with her boyfriend, Joseph, in Kimberly. James and his wife, Elaine, had settled in Victoria. Zan, recently returned from a working year in New Zealand, was also based in Victoria. Tim lived here in Alderlea with his girlfriend, Suzanne, but without a telephone. Peter offered to drive over and give them the bad news right after breakfast.

"What are you going to say to them?" I asked. "What am I supposed to say to the others? I don't know where to begin."

Whenever Alex phoned with something unpleasant he always started with, "Hi, Mom. Are you sitting down?" It had become a family joke which, this morning, stopped being funny.

"You'll know what to say when the time comes," Peter reassured me. "Be glad the kids can hear about this from somebody in the family. *We* had to find out from a stranger."

I knew he was right. A close, caring family member would know the best approach to use and the most helpful words to say…if only it didn't have to be me. This was going to be such a shock for everybody. I found myself wishing Alex had been struggling with a long-term illness. At least then we could all have prepared ourselves a little.

Extended family could be asked to spread this horrible news for us, and friends would tell other friends; it was a matter of phoning key people. There was no need to call anybody up at the Campbell River Reserve because the unknown cousin would have shared her story by now, but my First Nations friends who belonged to the local Tzouhalem Tribe would want to know what had happened. Business calls shouldn't be too complicated: Alex's Disability cheques must be cancelled, the various local services he used would have to be informed, and his apartment would need emptying.

A funeral would have to be arranged.

Alex didn't have a will and it would never have occurred to him to name an executor. Mom and Dad were listed as his next of kin only because there happened to be a pre-printed line on his wallet card. His latest girlfriend, a woman closer to my age than Alex's, had been on the scene for less than six months; we couldn't expect her to assume any responsibility. Tim, with all the good will in the world, was poor at being responsible. Zan had recently started a month of evening shifts in a brand new job. James and Elaine were flying to Hawaii on Friday morning. Kathleen was far away. Clearly, all the loose ends would have to be tied up by Mom and Dad.

1999

Finally, it was 6:30 a.m. and time to call Cricket. When she answered, I found that I did know what to say.

"Hi, Cricket. I have some bad news for you…"

This news was probably a lot worse for us than it was for Cricket. Her most acute grieving time had been three years earlier, in 1999, starting when her live in boyfriend, our Alex, first began having expensive late night drinking binges with his brother, Tim. After a few sleepy days and many complaints from Cricket, Alex invited me out for coffee; he said he needed an hour of my time for an important business discussion.

I had been expecting trouble because Alex had taken on too much. He was working many evenings at McDonalds to supplement the welfare cheque received by Cricket and the baby. He was going to school during the day, taking a college program, 'Home Care for the Elderly,' which was being financed by Tzouhalem Tribes. And on top of that, he was being a family man. Something had to give.

Alex began our 'business' discussion with a firm decision. "I'm planning to leave Cricket and Kaitlyn, and move in with Tim."

"Tim lives with two other guys and they share an apartment that has enough space for one, not four. Which bit of the floor will be yours?"

Alex ignored this. He assured me that he and Cricket had held detailed conversations and his leaving was "the right thing to do."

"What about all the girls that hang out at Tim's place? I think you're only looking for an excuse to party." That got a strong denial. All he wanted to do, he insisted, was find some peace and quiet, and get his own life sorted out. He wasn't going to party.

"Well, if you want my opinion,"—he didn't—"you should quit working at McDonalds and spend that time at home with Cricket and Kaitlyn. Kaitlyn is only eight months old. She needs you and Cricket to be with her in the evenings since you are both at school all day.

"You think Tim is out having fun while you are restricted," I continued, "and that's right, you are. But when you chose to become a father, you also chose to become restricted." This was a waste of my breath; Alex couldn't remember making any such choices. I tried a new approach. "Fathers have to find different entertainments than single guys. Fathers do fun things with their children, not with their brothers."

"Kaitlyn is fun for Cricket, not for me. All she cares about is that baby," Alex said resentfully. Not wanting to become involved in relationship issues, I changed the subject.

"What about finishing your college course?" Alex gave me a sheepish look and I pushed a little harder.

"You won't even get to school in the morning unless you are with Cricket. Tim isn't about to get up early and organize your breakfast and your books."

But Alex was sure he could manage—he had an alarm clock. Nowhere to do homework, no quiet for study, no encouragement to succeed, and a million distractions, but he had an alarm clock. It sounded as if school was already a lost cause.

"Well, I don't think this is the right thing to do," I said. "I think fathers belong with their babies. Fathers need to be responsible." Another waste of breath. Alex was unable, not unwilling, to assume long-term responsibility.

Before Kaitlyn had been conceived, back when Alex and Cricket first told me they thought they should have a baby, I had made my position clear: my first care and concern would be my grandchild.

Now I said to Alex, "I will be supporting Kaitlyn, whatever you decide to do."

He was very hurt. No one ever had to make guesses about what Alex was feeling—his emotions were always front and centre.

"Of course I love you, probably more than I love Kaitlyn. And we will visit the same as always." Alex smiled again and looked relieved, even though he could tell a "but" was coming "…But Kaitlyn is a baby and she needs lots of adults around her and I will be one of those adults and I hope you will be there with me."

"I don't know, Mom," said Alex. "I need some time to think about things. And Tim said he wanted me to come."

"Tim isn't a good influence on you," I reminded him. "He and his crowd are going to be in real trouble soon."

That was the only bit of the whole conversation Alex took in and processed. Not five minutes after I got home, Tim phoned.

"Hi, Mom. I just talked to Alex. Are the Boys in Blue looking for me?"

Tim agreed with me that Alex belonged with Kaitlyn; he said he had already told Alex to smarten up and stay with his kid. But then Tim always agreed with me. The trouble was, he agreed with everything everybody else said, too. And we both knew Alex wasn't thinking about Kaitlyn, or Cricket, or a place to live. He was thinking about partying.

Cricket phoned me twice a day after Alex moved himself and his possessions out of her apartment. He was keeping in touch, she said, and he was missing things like clean towels and regular meals and a comfortable bed. He made plenty of promises to "Come over and talk," but he never got there. The thing that hurt Cricket the most was Alex's lack of interest in Kaitlyn. "Alex better decide pretty soon in favour of his daughter rather than his brother," she told me. Alex's rejection was painful and, in her mind, it was also very public. "Everybody knows."

She and Alex shared the same group of friends, most of whom were either immature or neurologically challenged or both. These teenagers and permanent teens throve on drama, especially other people's emotional difficulties. Having dropped his college course within a week of moving to Tim's place, Alex now had time to think up lurid rejection stories. He was getting plenty of support while Cricket was feeling more and more isolated.

Of course, all the problems couldn't be blamed on Alex. Cricket admitted there were things in her life that needed to change. She was prepared to do the necessary work, but she thought they should be doing their work together. Sometimes it was hard for me to remember that she was only seventeen.

One night in March Alex finally dropped in for a visit with his little family. He told Cricket he wanted to come back home.

Cricket listed her house rules: no drinking, no drugs, spending controls, and a curfew. Alex became a tad less enthusiastic, but he still wanted to return, mainly because his whole welfare cheque had already gone into food for the multitude. He had no money left, and could she finance a trip to the bar tonight? "No." Well, could she loan him some money? "No." Well, could she pay for his cigarettes? "No." Well, could she buy him a new sweatshirt? "NO!"

Alex couldn't understand why Cricket was being so difficult. He decided she had too many rules, and he would stay with Tim.

Cricket told me it was hard to stick to her rules and not give in since she wanted Alex to come back. It was only because of Kaitlyn's future that she was toughing it out.

Through the early spring, Tim, still on probation, was being questioned regularly by the police. They suspected he and his friends were dealing drugs as well as using them. Alex swore he had no drug involvement, but Cricket said, "He sure has attitude."

Alex called me one day to announce Tim's latest news. The whole household would soon be evicted because of too many residents and too much late night partying. He didn't seem to understand that this was bad news for him, too. But he began to pay a bit more attention to Cricket and dropped in occasionally to see his daughter.

On a cool but sunny morning in April, Cricket phoned, asking if I could babysit for the day. Peter, who was leaving for work, took the call and had to tell Cricket that I had started a nasty stomach virus the evening before. This was unfortunate. Kaitlyn had conjunctivitis, and the daycare wouldn't take her, but, because of exams, Cricket *had* to go to school. In the end, she asked Alex to stay with Kaitlyn; she couldn't find anybody else.

Alex fed Kaitlyn her lunch and left food all over the highchair and mess all through the kitchen. He also fed himself—a whole pound of bacon.

He was supposed to have the baby at Cricket's school (a five minute walk away) at noon for her eye drops. He got her there at 1:30 p.m. and told Cricket she probably shouldn't use the medication as it was the wrong time.

Then he phoned Cricket at school at 2:10 p.m. "Kaitlyn's breathing is terrible. I think she is having an asthma attack."

Cricket had doubts—Kaitlyn had been fine half an hour earlier. But she couldn't see the baby and Alex sounded worried, so she said, "If she is all that bad, take her up to the hospital." This was another five-minute walk. Instead, without bothering to tell anybody, Alex made a late afternoon appointment with Kaitlyn's doctor at his downtown office.

When Cricket got home from school there was no baby, no stroller, no Alex, no note, wet floors covered with wet linen, and chaos in every room. Alex had gone through all Cricket's drawers and cupboards, leaving doors open and contents on the floor. He had also been through her bedroom even though he had been told to stay away from there.

Cricket phoned the hospital, and us, and any other places where Alex might have gone, trying to trace her daughter. She was starting to panic when Alex breezed in with the baby, who was fast asleep in her stroller. They had been to the doctor's office where Kaitlyn was described as "thriving" and Alex was described as "being paranoid."

Alex wasn't concerned, either by the doctor's comment or by the mess in Cricket's apartment. He said he had started to wash the dishes, but then had decided Kaitlyn needed a bath because some of her lunch was in her hair. He made a start on the bath, leaving the water running in the kitchen. Eventually, he heard the sink overflowing but by then the whole kitchen floor was wet. He left it like that, apart from throwing down most of the linen cupboard contents to soak up the water. The downstairs neighbours were complaining and Cricket, as well as being handed the whole clean up, had raised tiles in her kitchen.

Alex set forth a good reason for going through the drawers and cupboards and closets in Cricket's bedroom; he needed to find a dry pair of socks. He got his feet wet when he turned off the kitchen tap.

Apart from fury and exhaustion, Cricket's strongest feeling was anxiety. Kaitlyn, nine months old, had been left alone in the bathtub while Alex turned off the water in the kitchen.

"Alex is so careless," she grumbled. "I wish Kaitlyn hadn't got him for a father. I wish I had her with somebody else." So did I! Why did she think I had been pushing so hard all last year for birth control?

Cricket asked me to go to the courthouse with her on the following Monday morning. Considering Alex's many mistakes, his terrible lifestyle, and his lack of interest in his daughter, she had decided to ask the courts for full custody of Kaitlyn, supervised visits for Alex, and maybe even a restraining order. For her, the relationship was over.

My guilt, had I asked her to wait a few weeks, would have been impossible to live with because I knew her decisions regarding Kaitlyn were correct. But my guilt because of planning to help Cricket instead of Alex was almost as bad.

We were referred to a mediator who was employed by the legal system to help people work out custody agreements, in the best interests of the child, without having to go through the courts. This was considered the most productive way to go as long as both parties could co-operate. Whatever agreement Cricket and Alex decided upon together would be written out and placed in the Court Registry, making it legal and binding. If either one messed up, the other could go ahead with the Family Court option.

Cricket made it clear that she didn't want to limit Alex's access to the baby. "I wish he would spend more time with Kaitlyn. He could be playing with her at the daycare every morning."

Later that week, I had some quality time with Alex, who couldn't understand why everything was suddenly getting so complicated. He had excellent reasons and justifications for all his recent behaviours. "I thought it would be better for Kaitlyn if I left; it wasn't good for her to see her parents fighting all the time," and, "Tim wanted me to party, so I did."

Regarding his need for direction, Alex agreed his life was better when somebody else organized him and told him what to do. He said he didn't have a problem with having personal management at school and at work but he couldn't cope with Cricket constantly giving him orders.

"I know you think Cricket is bossy and controlling but don't forget you had the best eighteen months of your adult life with her," I reminded him. "And there's something else you could be thinking about. What if *Cricket* had been the one to walk away and *you* had been left with Kaitlyn for all this time!" But Alex wasn't able to see any point of view or appreciate any feelings except his own.

Unhappy about the idea of supervised visits, Alex told me it "wasn't fair" and there was no reason for Cricket to ask for that. He said he would never hurt Kaitlyn, and, since Cricket was worried about drugs, he would never take her to Tim's place.

I wondered, "Well, where would you take her, then? You can't wheel her around the mall for hours."

Waiting until I had his full attention, I continued, "Don't you think it's time you got your own place and started your life moving forward again?"

"I guess so," said Alex. "It would have to be shared accommodation. I can't afford to live by myself."

"Well, you have lots of friends. Find somebody Cricket thinks is sensible." Ignoring his protests, I went on, "You need a safe place to visit with Kaitlyn and you also need an extra adult around in case the phone rings or the sink overflows."

Cricket organized a family appointment with the mediator, and everything was arranged the way she wanted it—she thought—with full custody of Kaitlyn for herself and supervised access for Alex. But when the papers were delivered to Alex, he wouldn't sign them and take them back to the mediator's office. Thoroughly enjoying

Cricket's mounting irritation and all the attention he was generating for himself, he announced, "I'll see you in court."

"I'm going to get a lawyer," he told me. "That mediator is on Cricket's side."

"She doesn't take sides. The whole point of a mediator is an unbiased opinion." Trying to keep things simple for him, I explained, "She isn't there to make you feel good about yourself; she's there to make the best arrangement for Kaitlyn. And that's what you want too, right?"

Alex went through the list of things he couldn't understand.

I said, "But that's why you are supposed to be going back to the mediator by yourself—to get all your questions answered." Alex was silent; he knew I was right and he didn't like it.

"Don't forget," I reminded him, "you would have to pay a lawyer big bucks for her time. You can't do family things through Legal Aid." And—the first moment of truth—"Do you really want to pay for advice when you don't want to live with Kaitlyn anyway?"

For Alex, the thought of legal fees was disconcerting. He wanted a lot of excitement to build around his emotional upheavals, but he didn't want to have to pay for it. He changed the subject. "Why does Cricket have to have full custody of Kaitlyn, anyway? Just this week I found out I made a mistake and now I want her."

In other words, he found out about Cricket's new boyfriend. He didn't want Kaitlyn, or Cricket either, until somebody else showed interest.

It was time for the second moment of truth. "Cricket doesn't want any interference in her decisions about what is best for Kaitlyn from somebody who didn't care enough to stay at home," I stated.

"And that's exactly what the mediator told you, right? But it's easier to hear it from Mom because you know I care about you." We smiled at each other.

"This custody issue won't limit your visits with Kaitlyn. It'll be more like the relationship between you and me. We visit whenever we want to, and we can phone every day. That's the way it will be for you and Kaitlyn." At least that's the way I had hoped things would be. But in July, right after Kaitlyn's first birthday, Cricket decided to move to Alberta. Her mother lived in Calgary and the new boyfriend had family out there.

It had never occurred to Alex, when he left Cricket, that anything other than his own personal interests would be part of his decision. There was no thought of Cricket moving on without him. It didn't cross his mind that she might find a new man, or that she might leave town. Having no ability to see ahead to the possible results of his present actions, disaster always came to Alex as a complete surprise.

In the end, they parted on good terms. Alex told me he had signed the papers, giving Cricket full custody of Kaitlyn because she needed a better parent than he could be. By then he had two brand new nieces, twin daughters of his birth sister, Stephanie. He enjoyed being an uncle: it was all fun with no responsibilities. He suggested that Kaitlyn call him "Uncle Alex."

Passing the Torch

"I'm calling with some bad news about Alex," I told Cricket when she answered her phone. "He died last night."

She gasped. "I can't believe it!"

There weren't any questions. In the few moments we had to talk before it was time for her to leave for work, I shared some of the unpleasant details we had learned during the night, but Cricket didn't seem to be absorbing much. She repeated, "I can't believe it."

"I'll phone you tonight after Kaitlyn is in bed."

"Okay," said Cricket, and added, "I can't believe it."

Kathleen, our daughter, believed instantly. She heard, "Bad news," and was already crying before my next sentence: "Alex died last night."

She had several questions, the first being, "Do you think I should go to work today?"

"Yes. It's good to be busy at a time like this. Not only that, you need the hours."

Kathleen asked, "But when should I tell my friends?" Talking on the phone was her favourite occupation.

"Tonight after work would be the best time."

"I'm working ten till six today, and nine till five tomorrow and then on Saturday…"

"That's great, Kathleen." She had already shared her schedule with me earlier in the week. "Tonight you'll have time to phone all the people on your list."

More floods of tears. "But I can't phone Alex!"

"Don't forget, you and Alex had a nice chat last Sunday. He told me all about it. He said you called early in the morning and reminded him to phone me for Mother's Day. That was nice for me, and it will be something nice for you to remember."

"I guess I'll have to miss the funeral?"

"Well, I don't see how you could get time off at such short notice," I reasoned, but of all my kids with FASD, Kathleen had the least amount of reasoning ability.

"It's good that you have already arranged to come home for Corinna's wedding in August," I added hastily, giving her something else to think about. "When you get here, we can have a graveside service and bury Alex's ashes. James and Elaine will also have to miss the funeral; they are leaving for Hawaii tomorrow. A service later in the summer will be helpful for all of you."

Kathleen wanted funeral details.

"It'll be at St. Cecelia's, but I don't know what day," I told her. "Monday is a statutory holiday, so the funeral will probably be next Tuesday morning, but we'll talk again when it's settled for sure."

"I guess I'll have to miss it."

"Yes, you will. But we'll be able to do something else for Alex when you come in August."

"Where is Alex now?" asked Kathleen.

"He's at the hospital." I was thankful for the change of subject. "I think Dad will go up this morning; there might be some papers to be signed. Alex will probably be moved to the funeral home this afternoon, or maybe tomorrow morning."

"Won't he be at the church?"

"Not until the day of the funeral."

"I wish I could come home and go to the funeral."

"So do I," I said. "But we'll keep in touch. We'll talk on the phone again tonight. By then I'll know more about what's happening and you might have more questions."

Kathleen didn't know how to finish off a telephone conversation.

The rest of us had each developed our own way of bringing calls to an end.

"I'm going to hang up now because I still have to phone your brothers," I told her, "and Joseph will want to know why your mother is calling you so early in the morning."

"Bye, Mom, I love you."

Zan, a man of few words, let me do the talking. When I paused for breath, he said, "There's something wrong with my phone. You're fading away." The call finished with an abruptly cut off squawk. After a moment I called Zan again. His phone roared in my ear.

He shouted above the noise, "Hi, Mom. It's no better. I'll call you as soon as I get it fixed."

James answered the phone with a sleepy, "Hello?"

"Hi, James. It's Mom. Sorry to wake you up before your alarm, but I've got some nasty news."

"What's up?"

"Well, it's about Alex. He died in the night."

There was a long silence until James asked, "Is Dad all right?"

"Yes."

"What happened?"

I went through the few details we had been given for the fourth time. It wasn't getting any easier.

James asked, "How did you and Dad find out?"

"A policewoman came in the middle of the night," I told him, adding, "When I think of the many times we have had police cars parked in our driveway, and the cops looking for Tim…but this has to be the worst ever."

"What's next?"

"Dad is going to drive over to Tim's place right after breakfast to tell him in person," I told him, "and I have to do some more phoning. Uncle Bruce and Grandma don't know yet, nor the FASD folks, nor the church people." Those were all local calls. "And Dad has cell phone time to use up. He'll call Aunty Lucy in Chilliwack and anybody else who is long distance, and we'll email all the family in Holland."

"Anything else?"

"We'll have to talk to Father Joe at the church, and the funeral home people, and Alex's building manager. And the coroner is supposed to come over today. I never talked to one of those before."

"Can't be any worse than talking to a judge or a probation officer." James was trying to be comforting.

"Maybe not. I think Dad will want to go up to the hospital this morning to see Alex. He won't have to identify him, though. Somebody from Alex's birth family did that last night."

"Who was it?"

"I don't know. An older lady. Constable Gustafsson told us she was Alex's cousin."

"I'll bet she's one of those people from Tzou'in'quam Reserve up in Campbell River; they're always dropping in on Alex," said James. "Can Elaine and I do anything to help?"

"Could you call Zan in a few moments? Don't worry. He already knows about Alex," I tucked in quickly, "but his phone went funny while we were talking. He's going to phone me back, but he might not get through for a while."

"I'll call him before we go to work," James promised. "Do you want me to come up to Alderlea?"

"It would be wonderful if you could, but don't you have to pack for Hawaii?"

"I'll see what I can do," said James.

Right after breakfast, a nicely prepared meal we hardly touched, Peter drove over to the tiny duplex Tim shared with Suzanne. His knock woke both of them, but Suzanne stayed in bed. Tim came to the door, yawning. He was astonished to see his father so early in the morning.

"Tim, I've got some bad news for you."

Tim looked beyond his dad for the police, searching his memory for any recent misdemeanours and finding none. There were no police cars in the driveway, either. He looked back at Dad and felt a cold chill down his spine. Peter had tears in his eyes.

"It's Alex," said Dad. "He committed suicide last night."

"No," protested Tim. "No. No! It must be somebody else."

"They found him in his apartment."

Tim heard the words over again in his head, but they weren't as real as Dad's tears. He backed up a few steps and sat down heavily on the couch, feeling numb.

Peter came inside. "Do you want to come up to the house?" he asked. "Your mother would like to see you."

"I don't know," muttered Tim. "I guess so. Yes. I'll get changed."

Peter went through the house to the patio and stood with his back to the living room. His shoulders were shaking. Moving very slowly and still feeling numb and frozen although he wasn't cold, Tim dressed in the first clothes that came to hand. He forgot all about Suzanne, who, as she told me later, had buried herself under the blankets and was crying into her pillow.

I had almost finished my series of difficult phone calls when Peter and Tim came in. Tim was surprised to find everything the same as always, including my hug and Dad's offer of fresh coffee. But then he saw Alex's wallet, status card, and keys lying on the dining room counter. Tim looked at them for a long time.

"Those belong in Alex's pocket," he said. "I think maybe this nightmare could be true, after all." Giant teardrops rolled down his face; tears had always come easily for Tim.

The telephone rang. It was our first incoming call since Constable Gustafsson had phoned in the middle of the night, and tension filled the room. But this was one of Tim's friends calling us to see if the news he had heard could possibly be accurate.

Tim didn't mind sharing his tears and his disbelief over the phone and it sounded as though his friend was crying, too. The details surrounding Alex's death weren't very important to these guys. *That* had happened last night. How their crowd felt today was what counted. Peter slid Tim's coffee, thick with cream and sugar, into his hand.

This phone call marked the beginning of a day of almost nonstop telephone communication. We were glad Tim was with us because many of the callers wanted to leave messages for him. Tim took his calls in the guest bedroom; I took mine in my office. Peter, who hated telephones on principle, let us do most of the talking although he connected with his sister, and he did manage a few kind words for Suzanne when Tim checked in with her through their next door neighbour.

Mary Grace

Even though I deliberately kept myself busy, the morning seemed to drag on and on. Finally, it was nine o'clock and I could phone the hospital and talk to Mary Grace.

As the hospital's Pastoral Care Coordinator and Chaplain, Mary Grace helped many people who were coping with the stresses of grief and loss. I had been seeing her regularly as an outpatient for nine years, an unusually long time, while I fought the battle for my own health and, at the same time, struggled against the negative social currents that sent Kathleen, Tim, and Alex spiraling downwards into worse and worse situations.

Mary Grace had been a very important part of my life ever since the summer of 1993, when our tightly knit family unraveled into a group of strangers, awkwardly sharing the same house. According to general opinion, we became a dysfunctional unit because of Tim's criminal activities, but this time, general opinion was wrong. Individual family members' reactions to Tim's criminal activities changed our lives. And Mary Grace brought us safely through the changes....

Alex, an immature sixteen that summer of 1993, was very anxious about starting senior high school in the fall; as a result, he had lost his usual good humour. Learning how to drive was Alex's other obsession. He had to count on older siblings for his driving lessons because Peter had already used up all his teaching energy on those who came before, and I had flatly refused. I found Alex's driving terrifying.

We were seeing a lot of James, who was twenty. His home was in Victoria, an apartment shared with a girlfriend, but some of his part time jobs were in Alderlea. James had recently completed a course in MicroComputer Electronics Technology at CompuCollege in Burnaby and, as his proud mother told her friends, he had passed with honours. That summer he was a busy Computer Tech, holding down three part time jobs and looking for full-time work.

Kathleen had moved out of the family home two years earlier when she was twenty-two. She had managed to organize, all by herself, a small private rental suite and some minimum wage, full time employment in Victoria. She was able to make sensible financial decisions and we hoped she could cope successfully with independent living, but during her first month away from home, she met Adam. Adam had no charm, no intelligence, and no money, but he did have sex appeal and a remarkably good opinion of himself. Within a week he had moved into Kathleen's one person basement suite. Within another week she had been evicted. After that her life became a series of transfers into worse and worse accommodation, mainly to rid herself of Adam. Moves were followed by Adam's inevitable return, always with many promises to reform. Since Peter owned a truck, we were called upon to help with each change of residence.

One of our seventeen-year-old sons, Zan, had graduated from high school in the Class of 93 with seven bursaries to his credit and with plans to become a world class chef. He had already started his chef's training at Malaspina College in Nanaimo, living at home and commuting to school daily. On weekends, he worked at a local hotel as line cook. We met up with Zan face to face only occasionally, either very early in the morning or very late at night. Most of our communication was done through notes left on the kitchen counter.

"To Zan: Are you getting enough sleep?
From your worried Mother who hardly ever sees you and who hopes you are making nice lunches for yourself."

"To Worried Mother: Quit worrying.
From Zan who got 92% on Meats."

Our other seventeen-year-old son, Tim, had left home suddenly and unofficially in the middle of May. He didn't actually run away; he rode out of our yard on his bicycle and waved to me as he left. But he never came back.

At first he moved from friend to friend, telling the other kids' parents he had been kicked out. He showed up at the school sometimes, sharing alcohol and keeping in touch with all his buddies and his brother Alex, our paparazzi. But when the weather warmed Tim began sleeping outside, drinking heavily, and involving himself in thefts around the district.

Stress affected Peter and me in very different ways. Any family crisis enraged Peter, and of course Tim's escapades brought a series of calamities to our door. Tension at home mounted as the calls from school officials and then social workers accelerated, while visits from the RCMP became more and more frequent. The police officers were very kind to us and very concerned about Tim—a juvenile on the run. It was a scary summer. I soon reached the point of starting to shake whenever a police car turned into our driveway.

In early August, Tim committed the second crime for which he was charged—theft of a neighbour's truck. This brought mother and son into an even closer relationship as, together, we began to navigate the legal system. Eventually, the courts found Tim guilty and sent him on to a juvenile detention centre in Victoria. Peter, with his European background very much in the foreground, informed me that the family name had been dragged through the mud. We no longer had a son called Tim; he had ceased to exist.

But for Youth Corrections, with its cast of thousands, Tim's existence within one of their institutions was an important matter. We had calls from youth forensics, various legal system social workers, a child psychiatrist, a psychologist, a matron, a superintendent, and even a youth lawyer, all wanting family background and all concerned about Tim's placement after his time in 'Juvie' had been served.

Peter's temper stayed on simmer all that summer except for the times when it switched to high. Family members living at home were not allowed to mention Tim's name in his presence. He refused to deal with anybody from Youth Corrections and expected me to do the same. But I still had a son called Tim who was only seventeen and who needed to stay connected to his mom. And all those government professionals couldn't be ignored.

Back in early March of 1993 when life was calm, I had agreed to be assistant chief for the junior boys' week at Camp Columbia, a children's summer camp run by the Anglican Church. However, as we moved toward the end of June and it became apparent that Alex and Kathleen weren't managing well and that Tim was heading into serious trouble, I called to cancel. The camp people made me feel horribly guilty. They claimed to be unable to get anybody else; they were even willing to accept Alex as a junior counsellor in order to get his mother there. Going against my better judgment, I let myself be persuaded, thinking that this would at least be a week's respite from the telephone.

It was a good camp—the children were well occupied, busy, and happy, and Alex turned out to be an asset as a junior counsellor but, beginning with the first supper on the first day, I was unable eat. I couldn't lift the food and put it into my mouth. There weren't any alarm signals going off for me, at that point, although I did wonder what could be causing my difficulty. Maybe the noise and constant movement? There were more than one hundred people in the dining room for every meal, at least two thirds of them wriggling small boys. Maybe all the activities? As the week advanced we scheduled 'backwards lunch,' 'dress-up dinner,' 'utensil breakfast' and other favourites that made meal times fun for the campers but hectic for the adults in charge. Towards the end of the week, as well as not being able to eat, I discovered it was easier to go thirsty than to drink. Drinking was too much trouble. To me these were minor problems, a nuisance but not particularly worrying.

However, my 'inconveniences' were very worrying to the camp authorities. Before Junior Boys had ended, they escorted me to the Prevost Valley District Hospital in Alderlea, where I was stuck for a week, still unable to eat.

My doctor offered dietary and psychiatric supports, but the thought of talking to strangers about my eating problem was a lot more frightening than having an eating problem. If I had to discuss this difficulty with somebody official, before being allowed to go home, then that somebody should be the hospital chaplain who was at least slightly familiar. Her name was Mary Grace. She was about my age and, although we had never spoken to each other, I knew we both went to the same church and so we already had something in common.

Mary Grace and I became acquainted during two scheduled appointments.

Before my discharge from the hospital she said, "I want you to come back and see me again next week as an outpatient."

"Why?" I asked. There was nothing wrong with me, apart from my lack of interest in food, and that would surely right itself as soon as my life got back to normal.

"Just come," Mary Grace insisted.

She already knew what I still had to learn. The fight had commenced and the enemy had a name: Anorexia. By the time that summer was over I had dropped more than thirty pounds. But my eating disorder, even though it was very visible to others and a bit unpleasant for me, turned out to be a minor skirmish on the edge of the main battle.

Mary Grace told me, "There is something in your life that you just can't stomach," and "Anorexia is only a symptom of your real illness."

Soon there were other symptoms. Eye contact became impossible, especially in the mirror. The darkest, drabbest clothes in the closet were my automatic first choice. Particularly trying for my husband was something the doctor called sleep apnea. Peter was disturbed on many nights because I would suddenly find myself sitting up in bed, barely awake but coughing and choking and gasping for breath. My extensive reading habits changed from an enjoyable regime of fiction only to either non fiction or, preferably, no reading at all. I searched out the tucked away corner, the quieter room, the chair nearest the back and closest to the door. I'd do anything to get out of being the most visible last person in a lineup.

I avoided going to town by myself because of the doors and crosswalks. Public buildings usually have heavy doors marked with written directions: Push, Pull, Exit Only, Use Other Side. I would hang about in corners, nervously watching until somebody else went through the door, and I could be sure of getting it right. Crosswalks were worse than doors; they were right out in public. Waiting for a light to change or having a car stop for me became a terrifying experience. Jay walking, although dangerous, was a whole lot easier.

Meal times were also tricky. Peter and Alex, and Zan when he was there, wanted ordinary dinners at regular times. I didn't mind cooking for them, but I didn't want to sit at the table and eat with them. As well as having no feelings of hunger, I had no desire to be anywhere near a knife and fork although spoons felt safe. My dinner was always a cracker with either a bowl of plain broth or a smooth soup that had been put through the blender so that all the lumps were gone.

But from my point of view, the only difficult indication of illness started when speaking to people became much harder than listening to them. It wasn't a case of being unable to talk—I could answer questions, usually with one word. The hard part was in knowing where to start. So many new and traumatic things had happened in our family life, so rapidly, and there was so much to say about it all that my throat seemed to close, and I was weighed down into careful silence.

"You want to disappear," Mary Grace told me. She was right, but it was my emotions that disappeared. Except for fear, anxiety and guilt, which quickly became overwhelming, my ability to experience feelings was gone. The loss wasn't distressing. I hardly noticed any difference. A level internal life was a safe life.

"This is alexithymia," my psychiatrist diagnosed. "You can't feel your own emotions, anymore. It's because you are unable to share your feelings that you can't talk about yourself."

Years later, all of these symptoms were pulled together into one diagnosis, Complex Traumatic Stress Disorder, but back in 1993 the doctors were guessing. They had several different names for my illness: anorexia nervosa, mood disorder, anxiety disorder, depression. They said, "You are suicidal." Maybe I was. Certainly my present was frightening, and my future seemed to be right beside me all the time: huge and black and empty. But a person who is living without indignation or loneliness or irritability or sadness or any other feelings (except for fear and guilt—I was good at those) also avoids desolation and despair.

For me that whole summer was like walking along a tight rope and being overburdened with giant beach balls that had to be continually juggled. I lived in constant fear of saying or doing the wrong thing—of either dropping one of my balls or over balancing and falling off the rope. But everything could be managed, somehow, as long as I didn't eat.

Two decisions made by other people toward the end of September had devastating aftereffects.

Youth Corrections had already sentenced Tim to an eight month probationary period following his time in the detention centre. A juvenile usually served his probation at home under family supervision, but Tim's father refused to house him. I had to tell the judge, in a public courtroom, that my son wasn't allowed to live with us. The judge decided to place Tim at Outposts, a group home in down town Victoria for boys on probation. There was nothing good about Outposts.

While I was busy getting Alex started on a new school year, and supporting Kathleen's latest move, and attending all the court procedures and meetings necessary to establish Tim at Outposts, Peter decided, with no input from the rest of the family, it was time for us to move to a different neighbourhood. Heavy industrial traffic had been rerouted along our road for the last few months while the main highway was being repaired and Peter told us he could no longer stand the noise. It was a good excuse, but I knew what he wanted even more—to get away from bad memories. The truck Tim had stolen belonged to a farming family who lived right behind us, with whom we shared a fence. More than anything, Peter needed new neighbours who had not been ripped off by his son. He had also managed to convince himself that his wife's poor health would magically improve with a change of scene, never thinking the hard work and stress of moving could make a tricky health picture even worse.

On the first of March 1994, we moved from Prevost Bay, a few miles south of Alderlea, to Deerhome, a few miles west of the city. For me, this new place was 'Peter's House,' not home. On the day Zan, Alex, Peter, and I moved into it, James's relationship and living arrangements suddenly fell apart. Next morning, during a violent thunderstorm, all of his soaked belongings and sopping furniture were piled into the new living room on top of our things. Stressed and depressed, James organized himself into the last empty bedroom across the upstairs hall from Alex.

Kathleen began to realize that lucky James was established in the family's new home and she wasn't. Deciding she deserved the same privileges James was enjoying, she jettisoned Adam for the last time and returned to the fold, installing her enormous mess throughout the downstairs family room.

Meanwhile, Tim had stopped cooperating with his group home and the authorities there were threatening to offload him. Peter said firmly, "Not here!"

A few weeks after our move to Deerhome, my elderly cat died. He was too old to handle such an enormous change. As long as Sylvester was part of my life, I could manage our diverse household and cope with my ongoing anorexia, now controlled to the point where my body only lost a pound or so every month. But without Sylvester's warm comfort settling on my lap in the early morning and last thing at night, my drinking stopped again. Soon I was back in the hospital, this time for nine weeks on the psychiatric ward.

The lengthy admission didn't help much in terms of controlling my eating disorder (I lost more weight while I was there) but it was the beginning of a slow, gradual return to mental health. Away from my family's unusual and constant needs I finally understood that I was very ill, that getting well was going to be a long, hard struggle, and that Mary Grace could help me, but she couldn't do it for me.

And life moved on. Kathleen found herself a wonderful new man named Joseph, who was bipolar, learning disabled, and addicted to marijuana. Joseph quickly taught her to join him at the public trough; together, they somehow managed welfare fraud.

The mental health system, with its psych wards, psychiatrists, psychologists, and talk therapies claimed Alex. Even with strong home and community support, he was the first of my children to waste his welfare cheques, run out of money, and take up street living, although Tim quickly followed his example. Alex was also the first to be diagnosed with sexually transmitted diseases and the first to produce a child.

Tim's probation time at Outposts was the beginning of his life in the criminal sub-culture—a life of warrants, arrests, trials, probations, and imprisonments in various jails around BC. After he turned nineteen we could follow his illegal activities through headlines and police reports in the local newspapers. Between his many incarcerations, Tim needed my help to cope with evictions caused by partying with drunk and disorderly friends, and trips to Emergency whenever his drug dealers became impatient.

Mary Grace taught me healthier ways of coping with family disaster than giving in to anxiety and anorexia. Early on, I had memorized two of her mantras: "Nothing will change unless you change," and "The only person you can change is yourself." A mantra of my own had been added later: "Keep out of other people's relationships." As I learned to change, my family also changed.

Whoever could have guessed, back in 1993, that Tim and his father would come to a place of mutual understanding and enjoyment of each other's company? But they had, and now they were supporting one another through shared grief.

Mary Grace started her working day at the hospital a few moments earlier than usual that Thursday morning. By the time I called, she already knew Alex had died.

Her first comment was typical. "Ruth, what about Alex?"

My answer was also typical—a flat, unemotional, "You guys have got him. He's in your morgue."

We were both silenced.

Shock had made me totally focused and sharply aware of everything that had to be done. Although I didn't know it yet, shock had also caused most of my slowly returning feelings to slip back underground. Mary Grace, a person comfortable with all emotion including her own, was already grieving. It took us a few moments to come to a place where we could connect—Peter's desire to see Alex and Tim's need to see him. We settled on a time.

She asked, "Are you coming too?" but I had no interest in viewing the body, not even with Mary Grace close by, not even in the safety of the hospital chapel, one of my favourite places. I wanted to remember Alex as I had last seen him.

"Have you heard from the coroner?" asked Mary Grace. "I've got a note here to call her."

"She hasn't called us yet," I said. "According to Constable Gustafsson, she will be phoning sometime today."

"Are you okay, Ruth?"

"Oh sure, I'm fine," I said lightly. "All the kids know and Tim is here now. He and I are taking turns using the phone."

Mary Grace asked, "And is Peter all right?"

"Yes. He's planning a general email for all the people in Holland and he has already phoned Lucy and Fons."

"Oh, of course, his sister and brother-in-law in Chilliwack. I'd forgotten they were so close," said Mary Grace. "Would they be able to come over for a few days?"

"No. Lucy would come in a heartbeat, but she has surgery scheduled for tomorrow morning."

Another silence. Mary Grace tried again with, "Does your mother know?"

"Not yet." My mother would be ninety in another month; she was too elderly and too deaf to be receiving this sort of news over the phone. "I already called my brother," I added. "He'll be going over to her place at coffee time to tell her."

Clearly, I was fixated on details. Mary Grace stopped giving me opportunities to share my feelings and got down to business. "Do you know which funeral home you'll be using? You will need to get in touch with them because somebody will have to pick up Alex as soon as the coroner releases him."

I knew Generations Funeral Services had brought Alex to the hospital during the night and hoped they would be able to cover the next stage as well, but "release" was an unfamiliar term. Mary Grace explained the coroner's last duty. "I'll let you get on with your day," she finished. "I'll be thinking of you, Ruth. Don't forget we're meeting at 4."

We met in the hospital chapel on Thursday afternoons and my weeks were built around those appointments. I wasn't looking forward to going this time, but nine years ago Mary Grace and I had both made promises: barring illness or travel, we would always be there.

The Coroner's Visit

Of the two funeral parlours in town Peter and I preferred Generations because it was more familiar to us. Six months earlier when Willie, Peter's sister-in-law, had died, Generations' staff had been pleasant and easy to deal with.

Stanley Pierre, the First Nations manager of Generations answered my call himself. I found him remarkably helpful, probably because he was used to hearing from people who were experiencing the worst day of their lives. Having expressed his sorrow at the death of our son, whom he knew quite well, he confirmed that Alex would be collected from the hospital by one of his staff as soon as the coroner had released him. We could come in on Friday afternoon at 1:15 p.m. if that suited us, to make arrangements for Alex's funeral. He thought our family would need a day or two to discuss and plan.

I told him we already knew we wanted cremation for Alex and a funeral mass at St. Cecelia's Roman Catholic Church.

"You should call the church office this morning to get the date and time settled," said Stanley. "And if you want to have a reception there, you'll have to book their hall at the same time."

"Can you wait a second?" I asked. "I'll get a bit of paper and write all this down."

When I was ready Stanley continued, "Father Joe will want to have a meeting with your family to plan the service. Generations will take care of everything else. We'll talk about all that tomorrow."

If we wanted to publish an obituary, Stanley told me, we should bring it with us on Friday afternoon and Generations would organize getting it into next Wednesday's newspapers. I added 'obit' to my list.

"And when you come on Friday, please bring a bag of Alex's clothes for us."

"Clothes?" I asked.

"Yes, whatever you want him to be wearing at the funeral, and the viewing if you have one."

"We won't be having a viewing. And we won't be wanting an open casket, either."

"Okay." Stanley made a note. "Wasn't Alex on Disability?"

"Yes."

"Then you could call his worker," advised Stanley. "Social Services will cover some of the funeral costs."

That was the first good news of the day.

Sherry Foster, the coroner, phoned a short time later and introduced herself.

"I have to come and talk to you both; that's part of my job," she explained. "But I really *need* to come as well. I'm experiencing some confusion around this case."

She thought she could be at our place by about 10:30 a.m. and was pleased to hear that Alex's brother, Tim, would also be there.

Tim was less than pleased. He told us he wasn't going to talk to any strangers but he needed to know everything that was said. When the coroner arrived, and after we had turned the phone off and gathered around the dining room table, Tim settled himself in the living room where he could hear without being seen.

Hoping the coroner would understand, Peter explained, "Tim wants to be involved, but he doesn't want to see anybody right now."

I added, "He prefers to listen."

Sherry, who asked us to use her first name, was totally accepting. In her line of work, she told us, she often met people who needed a bit of distance.

"I was up in Alex's apartment last night," she began. "He had prescription drugs there but no sign of illegal drug use, and no alcohol."

We weren't surprised; we knew Alex was clean.

"There was some writing left on his table, but it wasn't exactly what you would call a suicide note. Did Alex keep a journal?"

"He doesn't have any one book that he writes in regularly," I said. "But he often jots down his feelings and thoughts on scraps of paper and he writes lots of letters."

Sherry nodded. "The apartment was a bit untidy but only from normal living. I would have expected either an enormous mess or, more likely, perfection."

"You would have found an enormous mess in Tim's apartment," I grinned, and was rewarded with a chuckle from the living room, "but Alex is pretty neat."

"Well, people who plan a suicide usually tidy up all their loose ends. Alex had laundry in his hamper and dishes in his sink. I'm missing something," Sherry fretted.

"Alex was born with a Fetal Alcohol Spectrum Disorder," I volunteered. "He has full Fetal Alcohol Syndrome."

There was a short pause. Then, "That explains it," said Sherry.

"We think Alex didn't intend to die; we think this was more of his usual problem of not understanding that behaviours have consequences," I explained carefully. It was always hard to know how much to share with the professionals. In the past, I had been very protective of Alex. Now, I realized, it didn't matter what I said. There was nothing left to lose.

"Alex hasn't got much impulse control. Nothing inside him says, 'This isn't a good idea,'" I told Sherry. "And he has quite a flair for the dramatic. A new person coming over for coffee would give him the perfect excuse to put on a bit of a show. He has staged several suicide attempts."

Peter said, "Too bad this time it worked."

"Or didn't," I commented, "depending on your point of view."

Sherry got out her pen and wrote a few quick notes. "When did you last see Alex?"

"Tuesday night at the Connecting Place," said Peter promptly.

"James took the whole family out for supper to celebrate my birthday."

Alex had been in a good space that evening. He and James had planned their father's party together because James had money, and Alex had First Nations status. Alex chose the Connecting Place, a popular Alderlea restaurant built on land leased from Tzouhalem Tribes. He presented his status card at the till so that James didn't have to pay any taxes.

"When we were leaving Alex gave me a hug," I remembered. "And I got a nasty look from an elderly woman who was sitting near the window. I warned, 'Don't look now, Alex, but there's an old lady right behind you, and I think she isn't happy that we were hugging each other.' Alex said, 'That calls for another hug!'"

Sherry smiled. "Good for Alex!"

"We had two family functions this week," Peter continued. "The kids were here last Sunday for Mother's Day. We went for a long walk with the dogs and then we had a big outside fire with hot dogs and marshmallows."

"Alex used my computer on Sunday afternoon to send this letter to his ex girlfriend and his daughter." I handed Sherry a folded sheet of paper. "Probably it was the last email he ever sent."

> Hi Cricket.
> Happy Mother's Day. How's it going? How is Kaitlyn? Tell her hi. Is there any way you can send me your phone number, so I can arrange to call you? Frankie and I are planning to come to Alberta sometime in June. Well he wants to do lots before his baby is born. My phone number is 250-758-8417, or my e-mail is Alexsb@hotmail.ca. So I look forward to hearing from you. I am not receiving your e-mails.
> Talk to you soon. Alex

"This is so typical of Alex," I said. "He often talks about going to Alberta, but it's all talk. He has never even reached the planning stage."

"Alex couldn't possibly organize something that complicated, the poor kid," added Peter. "He couldn't even organize a carrot cake."

Sherry raised a questioning eyebrow. I told her about last Saturday's phone call.

Alex had decided to bake a carrot cake, but he didn't have any cinnamon or cloves or nutmeg at his apartment. And he didn't want to go and buy all of those, he said, because it might turn out that he didn't like carrot cake and he would have wasted a lot of money. He wanted me to provide the spices for the first cake.

He read off the amounts of the things he would need and I wrote them down, then we gossiped for a while and exchanged news. At the end of the conversation Alex said, "Oh, by the way Mom, when I get the spices, can I have some carrots too?"

Sherry laughed. "Did he make his carrot cake?" she asked.

"Probably not," I said. "We both forgot on Mother's Day, so he didn't get his carrots and spices until I took them up to his apartment on Monday afternoon."

"And he was all right then?"

"He was fine. We had a cup of coffee together and a nice visit. Alex makes good coffee."

Sherry told us she had already talked to Mary Grace at the hospital, and so knew something of Alex's background.

"How old was Alex when you got him?" she asked.

I thought back to the day in July of 1978 when Alex had arrived at our house…

It was an early summer morning. Zanny and Timmy, both coming up to three and sharing a basement bedroom, were suspiciously quiet. Kathleen, who was nine that year, went down to see if they were awake.

She called up the spiral staircase, "Something's wrong, Mom."

I hurried until I got down to their room, where my feet stuck to the floor. My hands stuck to their sheets, their sleepers were stuck to their bodies, their mouths also appeared to be stuck shut. Even the curtains were stuck to the windows.

Zanny (it was always Zanny) had climbed out of his crib, visited Daddy's supposedly childproof workbench and discovered an enormous plastic container of office glue. How he managed to get it back to his bedroom and lift it into his crib we'll never know, but what he did with it after that was obvious. The only thing we didn't know for sure was how much glue had gone down each throat.

In those days, if a health problem occurred outside of regular office hours you were supposed to call the hospital Emergency, explain your difficulty, and tell them which medical clinic you belonged to. Hospital staff then got hold of the doctor on call for that clinic.

The doctor said, "I think you'd better bring them to Emergency. They might need a clean out. Bring the glue bottle, too. And don't give them anything but water for now."

Unfortunately, bringing them to the hospital meant bringing everybody. As well as our own four, we had two cousins, Ginny, ten, and Roger, seven, staying with us for a week. None of the children were old enough to be left at home.

Kathleen and I unstuck the little guys from their cribs and got them upstairs and into the bathtub, leaving the bedroom in a shambles. By that time their mouths had come unstuck and they were both calling for their breakfasts.

Ginny organized a bowl of cereal for each of the four big kids.

James, who was only five and not allowed to touch the milk jug, decided to help things along by pouring his own share all by himself. The milk slopped over his bowl and out across the table; his cereal travelled along with it. Ginny, who had been brought up to never waste food, sugared James's cereal where it stopped and made him eat it off the plastic tablecloth. That meant James needed a partial bath and clothing change before we could leave for the hospital.

In the middle of James's wash, the phone rang. It was Charles, our social worker, wondering if we could take a little boy for temporary foster care.

I asked, "Crib size or bed size? All our beds are full." Luckily, this child was crib size; he was only twenty months.

Charles said, "We're in Victoria at Children's Hospital, right now. We'll be at your place about 10."

"I hope we're back by then," I said. "We have to go up to the hospital right away, and maybe get two stomachs pumped. If we aren't at home, you'll know where we are. Use the backyard. There are lots of toys out there."

By the time the doctor had decided my toddlers didn't need to be cleaned out, all the kids were hungry, cranky, and totally bored with Emergency. They wanted to go and see Grandma. She was always good for cookies and juice.

"No," I said, breaking two granola bars into six pieces and handing them around. "We have to go right home because we are getting a new little boy this morning. He might be at our house already." Nobody was particularly interested although Ginny and Kathleen groaned dramatically at the thought of another boy.

Sure enough, two social workers, Charles and his driver, were already waiting for us when we got home, along with a sunny little fellow not yet walking or talking whom they introduced as "Alexander Bellman Jack."

Instant trouble. Zanny said, "*I* Alexander."

Timmy added, "*He* Zander."

I reminded them, "There are lots of Alexanders. Don't forget 'Mighty Alexander the Great King.'" That worked. Zanny ran to find his favourite book with Timmy, as always, right behind him.

Ginny brought the juice jug and a stack of plastic cups out to the picnic table. Kathleen, her black braids swinging importantly, followed with the cookie tin. James and Roger encouraged little Alexander to crawl over to the girls. He moved slowly with one arm held high at an awkward angle.

I said to the workers, "What about that arm?"

"It's fine now," said Charles, "but he had a bad break several months ago. His second cast came off last week. The nurses at Children's said he's so used to having his arm held up that it hasn't come down yet."

We completed the paperwork for Alex outside on the picnic table. It was a gorgeous day, and I didn't dare take those two social workers into the house, knowing how we had left the place: cereal all over the kitchen, sticky clothes all over the bathroom, and glue all over the bedroom where our new child would be sleeping.

"He was under two, and a temporary foster placement, originally," I told Sherry. "Kathleen and Tim came to us that way, too."

"Did you ever consider adopting him?"

"We did adopt him. He is legally our son," said Peter.

"Me too," came Tim's deep voice from the living room.

Sherry looked confused. "But 'Jack' is on his status card. And his cousin, who came to visit him last night, told us his name was Bellman Jack."

"Well, it isn't," Peter insisted. "His name is Alexander Bellman Spencer."

"The cousin who was there last night didn't know Alex," I soothed, "and Alex didn't know her, either. And because she was so late, they had no chance to become acquainted."

For Sherry's benefit, I added, "She was another in a long line of folks from the Tzou'in'quam Band in Campbell River trying to persuade Alex to 'come back home.' He doesn't particularly want to move to the reserve, but he likes all the attention."

We knew Alex had enjoyed going up to Campbell River for visits with his birth sister, his birth father, and especially his grandmother who always slipped him a bit of spending money. His Aunty Ellen who lived in our area, sometimes drove Alex back and forth. He had to listen to First Nations propaganda both ways, he told me, but that was okay because he liked Aunty Ellen, and it was a free ride. Many of his extended family, both on and off reserve, had made him feel very welcome.

Unfortunately, Alex's birth family didn't seem to understand that he was brain damaged. He looked good; he sounded good. Maybe they didn't know him well enough to recognize his disabilities. They had, they told Alex, found a place on the reserve where he could live, and now they hoped and expected that he would get on with moving there.

But Alex had no organizational skills. The actual shifting of bulk possessions from one place to another was beyond his capacity. Each change of residence he had experienced, so far, had been orchestrated by the women in his life. Even if he had wanted to live on the reserve, he wasn't capable of arranging a change of that magnitude.

"They have been pressuring him for ages," said Peter. "They were especially insistent a few years ago when his birth father, Victor, died."

"Alex said it was because he was Victor's oldest son," I explained. "They wanted him to follow all the First Nation customs: wear black-face and swim in the river early in the morning and change his diet because he was supposed to be grieving. And we were no help. We didn't understand what he was supposed to do."

"Alex didn't understand what it was all about, either," said Peter, "but he did try for a few days. Someone told him dark glasses could count as blackface. After that, he wore his dark glasses all the time, until he broke them."

"Somebody helped Alex with the paperwork for his status card, thank goodness. We didn't know how to go about sorting that out for him," I told Sherry. "Too bad they used the wrong name; it's actually illegal. We warned Alex that he might get into trouble over that, but he felt nervous about asking anyone to change it."

"It sounds as though he was putting some effort into maintaining a good relationship with his birth family," said Sherry. "Had he been in touch with them all his life?"

"Not really," I explained, "although we had sporadic contact with the biological parents when we first got Alex. His birth mother, who lived quite close to us, came twice with all her other kids. His birth father came a lot more often. Once his mother and father visited together, and on that occasion they brought Alex a bright red and yellow dump truck."

When Alex was four and a half, his Aunty Sandra and Uncle Edward applied to adopt him. They had put in an adoption application once before when Alex first became a temporary ward of the government, but Sandra's second pregnancy had intervened. In those days families weren't allowed to adopt until their youngest child was eighteen months old. Edward and Sandra truly wanted Alex. They started the adoption process again as soon as it was allowed but then, halfway through, they suddenly changed their minds.

"What happened?" asked Sherry.

We never knew exactly what happened…

Our social worker, Charles, brought the news one morning. "Alex's aunt and uncle want to adopt him."

I felt my face turn white—a horrid sensation. Although we had always known that other people besides ourselves wanted Alex, it had become very easy to think of him as part of our family.

Charles explained the Human Resources' method of progression, an approved system of gently weaning Alex away from us and familiarizing him with his new family in slow stages. First Uncle Edward and Aunty Sandra would visit him at our house. Then Alex and I would spend some time at their house. This was to reassure Alex that Mommy and Daddy knew where he was when he went there by himself, later on.

Child oriented day trips arranged by Uncle Edward and Aunty Sandra would follow, giving the cousins time to get acquainted. At first, Alex could choose a brother to take along; later, he would go alone. Soon he would be having overnight stays in Campbell River. These would be followed by a weekend visit and then he should be ready to move in with his new family. The social worker had recommended that Alex stay connected with us but further contact was always at the discretion of the adoptive parents.

"You should tell Alex today," said Charles. "That'll give him a few days to get adjusted before his aunt and uncle come. He needs to understand that they are visiting him, not you."

"Why don't you tell him?" I asked. "This is your idea, not mine."

"Oh, I'm sure you will do it much better than I could," said Charles hastily. "You're his mother, after all."

Alex and I dropped Timmy and Zanny off at the kindergarten at noon and continued on to the farm for our milk. Alex, who was always singing, filled the back seat of the van with "Old MacDonald had a farm." The farmer had phoned that morning with exciting news—there were two new calves in the barn next to the dairy. Alex and I would be the first to see them.

We lived in a rural neighbourhood. Although the younger kids had never seen a brand new calf, half grown cows were a familiar sight. I made the mistake of assuming Alex knew what to expect, but he thought a baby calf would be the same size as a baby kitten. The reality horrified him. I held him until he had stopped yelling and calmed down.

His first question was, "Where is their mothers?"

The farmer said, "She's in the other barn."

"Put it here, like me and my mommy," directed Alex. Clearly, this was not the right time to introduce the difficult subject of separation.

A better opportunity came later that afternoon. Alex was driving his little cars around the kitchen floor and singing to himself while I cut and baked cookies.

"Come and look at these, Alex." There were three cookie people lying on the counter: two large and one smaller. "That's you," I said, "And this is Aunty Sandra and this is Uncle Edward."

"Don't know those," grunted Alex indifferently. He poked at Uncle Edward's foot with a grubby finger.

"You're allowed to touch these three," I said, "because you get to eat them. But keep those dirty hands away from the other cookies. Uncle Edward and Aunty Sandra are nice people who want to meet you."

"Why?"

"They thought you might like to visit them, maybe for overnight."

"No," said Alex. "I like at home."

When Alex finally understood that he would have to visit with these strangers and eventually stay at their house without Mommy, he said through choking sobs, "I *hate* cow babies."

He never sang again.

We all cooperated with the method of progression. Aunty Sandra and Uncle Edward came to visit at our house and we liked them. A week later, Alex and I drove up to Campbell River, and Alex spent a happy afternoon playing with his cousin Tammy, who was also four, and little Ronnie who was not quite two. The social worker was present both times.

The following Saturday, Uncle Edward had a soccer tournament in Alderlea. Aunty Sandra came to collect James and Alex and she provided the lunch, but this was Uncle Edward's big day. James, who was eight and keen on soccer, had a wonderful time, but Alex was bored. Three weekends later, Alex was on his own with Uncle Edward and Aunty Sandra for the first time. They went to a beach. Alex enjoyed himself and he thought it would be fun to go to Tammy's house and stay for a night.

"That Ronnie-baby lots of cries," he told me. "But me and Tammy is big."

The first overnight was not a success; Alex came home exhausted. He said, "I didn't went to bed," and, "There was too much people."

Charles told me what happened.

The whole neighbourhood had come over "to see Bellman." Alex wasn't particularly shy but too many strangers made him nervous. He started crying for his mommy and eventually he fell asleep on the floor. Later on, somebody plopped him, fully clothed, into a bed. But Alex was used to an evening routine that included pyjamas, a wash, cleaning his teeth, a story, a prayer, being tucked in, and a good night kiss. As far as he was concerned, he hadn't gone to bed at all.

The second overnight was better. Aunty Sandra and Uncle Edward, at the suggestion of the social worker, had geared the time to Alex's needs rather than the wishes of the extended family. But when Alex came home, he announced, "Not going, no."

"Why not?"

"Staying home, I'm here," said Alex.

He was supposed to spend two nights at his uncle's place the next weekend. Charles planned to drop in on the Saturday afternoon to see how things were going. Alex's official move to Campbell River would take place during the following week.

The next Friday morning, when Uncle Edward and Aunty Sandra arrived, Alex ran to his bedroom instead of saying hello.

Sandra asked, "What's the matter?"

"I don't know," I said. "You'd better go in and talk to him."

They went into Alex's room, where the three of them had a long discussion. The rest of us stayed outside. Timmy and Zanny didn't like that a bit. They were five, nearly six, and always curious; they wanted to know what was going on.

Edward and Sandra came out without Alex. "He doesn't want to come with us," they said.

I considered going inside and telling Alex to march straight out to the car with no more nonsense but decided that wasn't my job. If Sandra and Edward wanted him, it was up to them to deal with all issues. Alex wasn't very big. There was nothing to prevent them from carrying him outside and putting him into their car whether he liked it or not.

I asked, "What are you going to do?"

"We'll try again on Tuesday," said Sandra.

I was tempted to say, "If you let him have his own way now, it'll be even harder next week," but again held my tongue. Alex was going to be theirs forever in five days' time; I had no right to interfere. Even though they were backing off the first time Alex was assertive, and even though I didn't see a whole lot of hope for their future relationship with him if they didn't take control now, it was still their choice how they handled things.

The social worker went up to Campbell River that Saturday as planned, and he had a lengthy discussion with Edward and Sandra, who said they felt unable to insist with this child. Firmness wasn't their way of parenting. They could see that Alex was happy with us and they were afraid he might not be equally happy with them. They told Charles they were nervous of his 'white' behaviours.

Two weeks later, they cancelled their adoption application.

Sherry said, "So then, you could adopt Alex."

"Yes, eventually," I agreed.

Alex's paperwork was geared toward adoption by a family member. He had to become a permanent ward of the court before anything else could happen. And since Tim was older and had been with us longer, his adoption had priority. Kathleen was officially ours by then, which meant we already had three children to support. We were able to start Tim's adoption before he turned eight and Alex's followed when Tim's was completed.

Sherry asked, "Did you see anything more of Alex's birth family?"

"Not for a long time," I said. "We exchanged a few Christmas cards with Sandra and Edward. I sent pictures of Alex once in a while and they sent pictures of Tammy and Ronnie. When Alex's adoption was completed they got one of the special cards James made on his computer, 'We have adopted a wonderful boy!' Apart from those minor connections, it was a twelve year gap."

"And the gap should have been a lot longer," said Peter bitterly. "We got caught in the middle of an adoption reunion when Alex was sixteen and we couldn't do a thing to prevent it."

"Sixteen!" exclaimed Sherry. "But adoption reunions aren't supposed to happen until the child is legally an adult and even then both parties have to agree. Adoptions are supposed to be protected!"

"We know," I said. "But we think Uncle Edward and Aunty Sandra thought Alex was still a foster kid. They and their perfectly gorgeous daughter arrived at our door one day. We hadn't seen them since Alex was four and nobody in the family except me knew who they were. Too bad I couldn't have met them at the gate. How could I ask them to leave right in front of Alex?…and he was totally smitten within seconds. He couldn't believe that such a beautiful girl, whom he didn't even know, had actually come to visit him.…"

We all sat around the kitchen table drinking tea and eating homemade cookies. The conversation was general but a bit stilted: the weather, the government, the planned improvements for the Island Highway, another soccer tournament, this time with Ronnie, now fourteen, playing. Like us, they were still living in the same place.

Again we found Uncle Edward and Aunty Sandra to be exceptionally nice people, soft- spoken, gentle, and accommodating. They didn't say why they had come, but they asked if they could come again sometime. And they suggested to Alex that he might like to go to Campbell River and see his birth father and his grandma, who lived together.

Peter and I had always liked Victor, Alex's birth father. He was a friendly man who, like Alex, needed a bit of extra mothering. I remembered supplying him with Band Aids during one of his visits to Alex, and on another occasion, he wanted me to cut the cuffs off his new jeans because they were too long and he was walking on them. He wasn't a well man, even then. Each time he came, he seemed weaker than the time before. At first, he used a cane, then two canes; the last time we saw him, he had a walker. Uncle Edward said, "He's in a wheelchair now, and has been for a long time."

Aunty Sandra phoned Alex several times over the next few months. She and Uncle Edward still hoped he would come for a visit and meet his father and grandmother and his sister Stephanie. Alex liked the idea of having a whole other family, and he was pleased that they wanted him but nervous about taking the next step. It was early December before he finally decided to go.

Peter was totally in favour of Alex getting to know his birth family; he didn't want me to have any doubts. But I knew the timing was poor and my son's stress levels were already high. He was struggling with the shift from junior to senior high school and, having failed his first driving test, was booked for a second early in the new year. All the excitement connected with Christmas, plus the family move to a new house planned for the next February, had him thoroughly stirred up. He was unusually immature for someone recently turned seventeen.

He came back from Campbell River overwhelmed with his day and his birth family and all the gifts he had been given, but he didn't understand that he was being welcomed *home*. Some of the aunts cried over Alex and told him how much they had missed him. He loved it. He told us about "my sister" and "my dad," which I found a bit hard to take, at first, but Peter didn't seem to mind.

Uncle Edward sent us a lovely message—he said it was a good thing he and Sandra hadn't adopted Alex when he was four, because at that time they had not yet stopped drinking and partying. He thought we had done a great job.

"That was very nice of them," said Sherry. "And it's awesome that Alex's two families got along so well. It must have made things much easier for him.

"Now, there's something else I wanted to ask you about. Alex obviously spent a lot of time at the hospital. Last night all the people there seemed to know who he was, especially the Emergency staff. Why was he so often on the psych ward?"

"Officially? Suicidal and depressed."

"He wasn't suicidal," said Peter, "but he wanted lots of attention."

I told Sherry about the first 'attempt.' Late one night, at the place where he was boarding, Alex had swallowed a handful of pills. He had then knocked on various bedroom doors, announced what he had done, informed the gathering family of his need for an ambulance, and had gone quietly back to bed, where he waited to be rescued. Somebody from the household took him to Emergency.

"But that's not attempting suicide," I said. "Peter is quite right. That's dangerous attention seeking and Alex did it often."

In fact, I finally told him there were better ways of getting admitted to the psychiatric ward than doing the pill thing. If he honestly wanted to be there, he should go down to the city park beside the train station and take off all his clothes. He'd be welcomed in by the psyche ward staff mighty quick and it would be a lot easier on his family and his liver.

Sherry smiled, "You didn't!"

"I did." Seeing her interest, I shared another story. Right after one of his 'attempts' I had visited Alex on the psychiatric floor and the first thing he said to me was "Mom, you have to get me out of here. I have to go to a birthday party."

I told him he could either die or he could party; he couldn't do both. This time he had chosen to die; now he had to live with the results of that choice, and one result was going to be missing a party. Maybe next time he would choose the party, instead.

From the living room, Tim called, "Alex didn't get it."

"He couldn't get it," I sighed. "He was born with a lot of damage in the part of his brain that understands risk taking and death."

Alex had poor judgment, poor impulse control, poor reasoning ability, a poor memory, and no understanding of consequences. He was, I told Sherry, a walking disaster area. He never had a chance.

"Not only that," I added, "there are lots more people like him out there, with exactly the same deficits."

"I know it," agreed Sherry. "I think FASD is often a factor in suicide. It certainly was in Alex's case. I don't think he had any intention of killing himself." She looked straight at me. "I think it happened because he was slight, and poor at balancing, and the shower bar didn't fall until it was too late." She put the lid on her pen. "Unfortunately, I can't write 'accidental death' when it's a suicide, but I do think this death was the closest thing to an accident that a suicide could ever be. It wasn't a planned event."

She opened her case and started putting away her notes. "Are you using Generations Funeral Home? I'll release Alex to them, probably first thing tomorrow morning. And are you going up to the hospital to see Alex later today?"

"Yes," said Peter. "Tim and I are going right after this."

"Don't you want to go, Ruth?"

"No."

"Well, can you tell Tim that he won't have to go downstairs to the morgue? Mary Grace will bring Alex up to the chapel. She'll stay if you want her to, or you can be there by yourselves."

As Sherry left she added, "Phone me if you have any questions. And I'll call you in a few days to see how things are going."

An Underground Spark

It was nearing noon when Tim and Peter drove to the hospital for a last visit with Alex. Tim was tense, and shaking again, but he had stopped crying and had determined to see the thing through. Afterwards, during a lunch he couldn't eat, Tim told me about their viewing.

Mary Grace met them at the main entrance of the hospital and took them around the corner and into the chapel. Alex was already there, lying on a stretcher. He was wearing a dark shirt, but only the collar and the two top buttons showed. The rest of his body was covered with a hospital blanket.

Peter put his hand on Alex's head and said, "Lexie-Ally."

This was one of the nicknames Peter had often used for our boys, along with "Gucks" for James, "Mack" for Zan, and "Tintin" for Tim. Hearing Alex's old name brought back Tim's tears. He looked at his brother and touched a cold hand under the blanket; then he went out to the lobby to wait for Dad.

Peter stayed a few moments longer, praying and being with his son for the last time. "I thought Alex looked pretty much the same as always," he told me later, "except for the mark around his neck."

When Tim and Peter were ready to leave, Mary Grace gave each of them a hug. Tim said, "I touched him."

"That's good, Tim," commended Mary Grace. "That's what you needed to do."

"Yes. If I hadn't seen him and touched him I would never have believed it," Tim admitted.

As soon as Peter and Tim had gone to the hospital, I phoned the Ministry of Human Resources. My usual way of doing things was to avoid important phone calls for as long as possible, especially if they involved contacting a stranger and even more especially if that stranger was part of a government ministry, but I had never been as focused as I was that morning.

Because of speedy staff turnover rates in Social Services, the name of Alex's latest social worker was a mystery. Their receptionist told me it would take a few moments to track down the right person.

"Are you a client?" she asked.

"No. I am the mother of a client."

"You do understand that our staff are not allowed to give out any personal information about our clients?"

Of course I understood. I had been advocating for my children for the last thirty years, first with the medical system and public health, then with the Ministry of Education, and later on with the legal system, Corrections, Welfare, Disability, Emergency, various drug and alcohol services, and the many little branches of mental health. No government system will ever disclose the inside story on an adult client, not even if the adult in question is a permanent teenager and it's his mother needing to know.

Eventually, a man's deep voice came on the line.

"Hello, Mrs. Spencer. This is Ken Johnson, Alex's worker. How can I help you?"

"I called to let you know that Alex won't be on your list any longer. He died last night." Ignoring his horrified gasp and pending interruption, I hurried on.

"I was talking to Stanley Pierre at Generations Funeral Home this morning and he said I should get in touch with you. He thought, since Alex is on Disability, Social Services might pay some of the funeral and burial costs. Is that right?"

"Yes, that's right, although there are some conditions," said Ken. "But I am so sorry to hear about Alex." I wasn't going to be able to avoid the little chat after all.

"He was here last week and we talked about his new apartment and his new girlfriend. He was fine then. What happened?...a car accident?"

"Suicide," I said almost inaudibly.

"No! Not Alex!" said Ken sharply. "He wasn't down. He's been in good shape for a long time." He paused to collect himself. "Well, I'm very sorry to hear this," he repeated.

"So were we," I said flatly, clearly discouraging further comment.

Ken kindly moved on. The ministry would pay for all the basics except the death certificate, he told me, but they wouldn't cover any extras. If we wanted an obituary in the paper or music and flowers at the funeral or a reception or a grave marker, we would have to handle those ourselves. But they would accept the bill for the storage, transportation, and preparation of the body. They would also attend to the costs of the casket and the funeral service. For a full burial, they would pay for the space and the opening and closing of the grave. For a cremation, they would take care of the crematorium fees and up to $200 for a permanent funeral urn.

"In exchange for doing all that, we will ask you to relinquish Alex's death benefit."

"Done," I said, knowing that we would be getting the best of the deal. "That's generous of Social Services, and it will make things easier for us."

Death benefits are based on Canada Pension Plan payments. Alex had held short term, part time, low paying jobs throughout his working life, and I knew he had not contributed much to CPP. Even if his death benefit was more than my vague estimation, we were being offered both support and convenience. It was an easy choice.

Peter and I had been living on a careful budget ever since Peter's retirement. We knew, because of other recent deaths within our extended families, that even a small, quiet funeral would cost about three thousand dollars. However, we thought this funeral might be bigger, considering the numbers of young folk already calling Tim. We had been concerned because an appropriate send off for Alex would have to be paid for with plastic money, something we seldom used. But with Social Services covering all the basics, we could afford the extras.

Early that afternoon we finally found the time to send a general email to Peter's siblings in Holland. Neither of us had been looking forward to the exercise.

Peter, who always did his best to avoid any kind of writing, scribbled off a short note and brought it to my office. I could usually read his handwriting although his spelling was entertaining. His capital letters were hard to decipher as they were always formed in the old European way, even when he wrote in English. But this message was all in Dutch. My only knowledge of Peter's mother tongue was a few spoken phrases learned from my sister-in-law, Lucy.

I knew how to use a keyboard, email, and internet but had never learned to type. For me it was always the slow hunt and peck method. Peter had no knowledge of the ways of computers but he did know how to use a typewriter. He couldn't believe the length of time it took me to finish and correct each Dutch word. I hadn't a clue what I was telling Peter's family about Alex's death.

And of course the telephone kept interrupting us.

By the time our general email was ready to go out, we were straining to be polite to each other. I clicked 'send' as Tim interrupted his latest telephone conversation to yell, "Hey Mom! James is here!"

"Perfect timing," said Peter. He went to put the kettle on.

James was pale. His eyes were red rimmed and his hands were shaking. I wondered if he had asked to have the afternoon off, or if the suggestion had come from his work place. He and Tim had a quiet visit in the living room while Peter turned the telephone volume control to low and made tea. I got out the cookie tins for the third time that day. So far, my delicious homemade cookies and squares hadn't been touched.

Over his hot cup, tightly clasped in both hands, James shared a new problem. He and Elaine hadn't purchased any cancellation insurance for their trip to Hawaii.

They had married quietly in the fall of the year 2000 and had celebrated this event with a huge wedding reception nearly a year later in the summer of 2001. Now, in the spring of 2002, they were taking a well earned and richly deserved vacation: five days of touring around the Hawaiian Islands followed by a slow cruise home. They were calling it their honeymoon and, knowing he needed a complete break, Elaine wasn't allowing James to bring anything connected with work, not even his laptop.

"We're supposed to be leaving tomorrow afternoon," James said, "but it's hard to decide what to do. If we don't go, we'll lose all our money. If we do go, we'll miss Alex's funeral."

"If you are asking for my opinion, I think you should go," I told him.

"Honestly?"

"Yes. I wouldn't have said that if Alex had been terribly ill and had asked you to stay," I explained, clarifying my position. "But now the deed is done and none of us can do anything more for him. Cancelling your trip won't change a thing. Dad and I will miss you and Elaine enormously, but Tim and Zan will be here to help."

"I guess so…" James sounded dubious.

"You won't be the only ones not there," said Peter. "Aunty Lucy and Uncle Fons can't come because of Lucy's surgery tomorrow. And Kathleen's holiday isn't until late in the summer."

"Dad and I want to have Alex cremated," I added. "We'll bury his ashes at a graveside service in August when Kathleen is home and Aunty Lucy is better and you and Elaine are back. Mary Grace might do the service for us; I'll ask her this afternoon."

James looked relieved. "Okay," he said. "That sounds better. If we're all there, and Mary Grace, too, I won't feel so bad about missing Alex's funeral. Where will he be buried?"

"At St. Matthew's," I said. "That big graveyard along the road from St. Cecelia's, the one with all the trees that looks like a park. We have lots of ancestors there already and that's where Dad and I want to be planted."

"Aunty Kath is buried there," Tim suddenly remembered. "Dad took a video of Poochie walking on her grave. Alex would like to be there; he always liked old ladies."

James smiled for the first time. "Alex used to take their coats and help them go and sit down and they always thought he was wonderful…and he thought he was, too."

"Why don't you guys go out and get some exercise?" I suggested, slipping into mom mode. "You could take the dogs for a walk. I have to get ready to meet Mary Grace and your father would like to have a rest. He was up half the night."

James and Tim leashed our three wildly excited dogs, got them all moving in the same direction, and headed for the river. As I followed them out of the yard a speedy little red car zipped past mine with someone who looked very much like Alex's Aunty Rhonda behind the wheel. Through my rearview mirror, I saw the car turn into our driveway.

I considered going back but decided against it. There was no point in making myself late. Peter could talk to Aunty Rhonda, if it was Aunty Rhonda, without my help.

The Chapel

The hospital chapel, small and noisy, was the room where I had first been heard, the room where I had learned to know myself. Long ago, I had written a poem about this special place. It began:

> In the midst of intrusive P.A. calls
> and pneumatic tubes crashing through the walls,
> and urgent feet up and down the halls,
> we meet in a sanctuary of peace.

That afternoon, to my surprise, everything in my refuge looked the same as always. The ten comfortable chairs…the long table covered with a heavy white cloth…bright sunlight shining through the stained glass window…even the pictures were hanging in their usual places. My life had slipped sideways; it seemed strange that the chapel hadn't changed.

How many times during our bad years had Alex met me there? He knew I was usually early for my counselling appointments and Mary Grace was usually late, and so he chose Thursday afternoons to share his problems, to 'borrow' money and to introduce new girlfriends. Often, by the time Mary Grace got to the chapel, I was worn out and more than ready to be rescued.

Eventually, Mary Grace spoke to him in a way that even Alex could understand. "We both love you, and we like to see you but not here. Your mother needs some quiet time before her counselling time. Her Thursday afternoons belong to me!" Not that Alex stopped coming, but his visits were fewer and much shorter. He made sure he left before Mary Grace arrived.

For me, seeing Alex dead in the chapel would have been a terrible mistake because that's how I would have always remembered him. Now I could picture him beside me, sharing jokes, chatting about his week, and constantly checking his watch so that Mary Grace wouldn't catch him.

Mary Grace set the agenda for our Thursday counselling sessions; she had been quite right in telling Alex this was her time. From the beginning, she had been firm—no planning ahead on my part. During each week I composed a daily journal of events and opinions, changes and questions, poems and drawings and the occasional glued in newspaper clipping…anything interesting, important, or alarming for me. On Wednesdays my journaling pages were left in Mary Grace's folder at the hospital, giving her time to read and think about my issues. Then on Thursdays our sessions went her way.

Sometimes that could be scary and my stomach was often roiling before our time together. But Mary Grace said real change was usually frightening. If I wasn't a bit nervous coming to our chapel times it meant my counselling was starting to be fun and no longer necessary.

Entering the chapel that Thursday afternoon, I closed the door, turned off the overhead lights, and dimmed the lamps. When Mary Grace came in, she allowed the missing overheads but switched both lamps back on and enveloped me in one of her special hugs.

"Hello, Ruth," she said. "Were you remembering how Alex used to meet you here?" Over time I had become used to Mary Grace knowing what I was thinking. She always knew.

She sat down beside the brighter lamp and smilingly indicated the chair next to hers. I dropped to the floor at her feet instead. There was too much light in her corner and this was not a good moment for eye contact.

"Peter and Tim didn't stay very long this afternoon, but I think they had a good visit with Alex. It was nice to see them," said Mary

Grace. "How are things going for you?"

"Reasonably well," I answered. "It's all brand-new experiences and a bit overwhelming. I hope I'm doing everything I'm supposed to do."

"Knowing you, you're probably doing more than anybody would expect. But this is a time to think about you, not about everybody else. It's a time to let yourself be supported."

I felt her sharp look as she added, "And don't forget, Ruth, you need to eat even when it's difficult. You have come so far; we can't let all that hard work go to waste. The most important thing right now is taking care of yourself."

"I knew you would say that," I said, finding comfort in the familiar. "Actually, nobody in the family is eating very much."

"That's understandable," said Mary Grace. "Alex's death has changed all of your lives so suddenly. Tim was having a hard time when he came to see Alex. How are the other kids doing?"

After nine years of being my counsellor Mary Grace knew all of us very well indeed. I shared details of my early morning calls to Cricket, Kathleen, Zan, and James, and added, "James is at our place now. He and Elaine are leaving for Hawaii tomorrow."

"Are you okay with that?"

"I told James he should go." I felt pins and needles starting up one leg and wiggled my foot. "But since they will miss Alex's funeral and Kathleen will too, we are all hoping you will be able to help us with a graveside service later on."

"Of course! I would love to do that for Alex."

"I'm glad," I murmured, risking a quick smile in Mary Grace's general direction, "because lots of people who can't come to the funeral have already asked. Peter's sister, and another friend who broke some bones in a bad accident and isn't allowed to drive for a few months, and our niece can't get away without two weeks' notice."

"Funerals never come at convenient times," said Mary Grace. "Speaking of times, has the church given you a day and time yet?"

"No. We're hoping for next Tuesday morning but that hasn't been confirmed."

"They should have called you by now." Mary Grace was always

one step ahead. "Have you and Peter had a chance to think about the funeral service?"

"We chose some hymns and Bible readings early this morning," I said. "Alex's friend Frankie has already offered to be a pallbearer. And we've asked Linda and Rachael, from our church, to do the music."

"You've made a good start. And how did things go with Sherry? I'm glad you have her for your coroner; she's one of the best."

"We liked her," I said. "She was understanding and easy to talk to. The only hard bit was that she wanted so much history. She stayed for a long time and stirred up a lot of my old memories."

"Anything you need to share?"

"Nope. There wasn't anything you and I haven't talked about already, except for…" I needed a moment to pull my next sentence together. Mary Grace waited quietly. "Sherry said it was an accident," I blurted.

"I was hoping you would be able to tell me. Do you want to say anything else?" I shook my head.

"Do you need me to ask you about it?" I shook my head again. This was a technique Mary Grace had developed years ago when I had first lost the ability to talk about my own things. She had become skilled at asking the right kinds of questions—questions that needed only "Yes" or "No" for answers. These days, I was usually able to contribute in a normal way during an ordinary conversation.

We discussed Sherry's work, her responsibilities, and her knowledge of FASD. I began to realize how easy it had been to deal with that rare being—a legal system professional who actually understood my kids' problems.

Mary Grace changed the subject. "What about Generations? Did you get hold of Stanley?"

"Yes, and he was helpful. He said Social Services would help pay for the funeral of anybody on Disability. He said I should call them."

"And?"

"I did and they will."

"Good," said Mary Grace. "Have you been up to Alex's apartment yet?"

"We're going tomorrow. Stanley said we should get…" I stalled again.

"Get what?"

After a short struggle for words, I muttered, "Good clothes for Alex."

Mary Grace touched my shoulder. "This isn't something you have to do yourself, Ruth," she said gently. "Maybe Tim and Peter could do it together? Or could your brother go?"

"I won't mind being at the apartment—at least not much," I said. "It's thinking about all Alex's belongings that's hard. But I need to be there because we have to get the *right* clothes. No matter where he's going, even to his own cremation, Alex will want to be well dressed."

"Spiffy." I could hear a smile in Mary Grace's voice. "That's how Alex always looked. It's hard to believe we won't be seeing him like that anymore."

She leaned back in her chair and went on, "You know, Ruth, Alex spent a lot of his time here and everybody in the hospital will miss him. He was so well known around this place."

"Yep. Emergency and psyche ward, his favourite places to be." I shifted into a more comfortable position. Now that we were talking about Mary Grace's reaction to Alex's death, I could face her but the floor still seemed safer than a chair.

"Yes, and the Emerg and Psych people are upset," Mary Grace confirmed, "but it's not only those."

Peter had been the gardener at Prevost District Hospital for nearly thirty years. Many of the maintenance staff and other hospital employees, who had worked with him before his retirement three years earlier, had already approached Mary Grace, their hospital chaplain, needing to express their sorrow regarding Peter's loss. They were all feeling badly for him.

"And lots of switchboard and reception people know you, Ruth, from seeing you here most weeks and they know Alex is your son."

When Mary Grace had arrived at work that morning, she told me, the switchboard operator kindly took her aside and told her what had happened. Then, right after my phone call, Mary Grace had gone up to the psychiatric ward.

The Chapel

"I needed to talk to somebody about Alex's death," she said. "The nurses up there knew him so well."

Phil Chong, the head nurse on Psych, had listened and then asked Mary Grace if she wanted to see Alex. They went down to the morgue together. Mary Grace hugged Alex with, "Oh Alex. Why did you do this?" and Phil said, "He's a handsome young fellow, isn't he? He looks Spanish." Mary Grace thought their little viewing had helped them both.

"I was struggling to believe that Alex had actually died," she said, "and I think it was like that for Tim, too. But you accepted his death instantly, didn't you, Ruth?"

I nodded.

"Well, that's a bit unusual, but for you it makes sense," said Mary Grace. "When emotions aren't there to help you through, sadness gets reduced to hard facts. Do you remember all the work we did on the stages of grief?"

"Yes, I do." Pins and needles again, I wiggled my other foot. "And I would love to indulge in denial but with the police at the door, denial is more a luxury than an emotion. And anger doesn't happen very often for me, and so far, I'm not feeling sad."

"You aren't feeling anything. Your emotions are all there, but they're temporarily subterranean, and that's okay. Probably you'll start to notice some sadness in a few weeks; when that happens I want you to phone me, even if it isn't our regular day."

"Can you tell me about the police at the door?"

I told Mary Grace about our time with Constable Gustafsson. "Alex died at nine o'clock in the evening," I finished, "and she came to us at three o'clock in the morning. Since it was already six hours after the fact, I wish she would have waited till a more sensible time."

"I wish you would have called me while she was still there," said Mary Grace.

"In the middle of the night? I couldn't."

"Yes you could," she corrected firmly. "I'm sorry you didn't. I could have come out to your place and helped you through the police visit; I would have been happy to do that. If anything like this ever happens again I want you to call, no matter what time it is."

"I hope nothing like this ever happens again. Once is enough." My voice cracked and faded. Mary Grace reached over and took my hand in hers.

"You know, Ruth, it's been ages since you've had to darken the room and sit on the floor," she said. "Not that I mind if that's what you need to do to get through this, but I'm crying and I wish you could cry, too. I wish I knew how to make that happen for you."

So did I, but my crying had vanished years ago. It wasn't a matter of suppressing tears —they weren't there to be suppressed. I had somehow lost the ability to cry. And for Mary Grace, who always had to ask the right questions, or make guesses about what I might be thinking, coping with tears would have been much easier.

We sat silently, holding hands, and I could feel myself relaxing. After a while, Mary Grace said, "When he found himself in Heaven, nobody would have been more surprised than Alex," and we both laughed.

Mary Grace looked at my watch. "I'll have to go soon; there is a meeting upstairs in five minutes. After that I'll be away for three days. But Monday is a holiday—what if I come out to your place on Monday afternoon? We could have a nice chat and maybe go for a walk together."

"I would like that," I said, grabbing the arm of the chair and slowly straightening my stiffened body into a standing position. Everything hurt. I was much too old to be sitting around on floors.

"We have time for one more hug," said Mary Grace.

The Sparks Begin to Fly

The guys were outside enjoying a beer when I got home. I poured myself an iced tea and joined them on the front porch.

"Glad you're back," James greeted me. "Next time the phone rings, it's your turn to answer."

Peter didn't waste time on a greeting. "A lady came to the door right after you left, asking questions about Alex's funeral," he told me.

"We saw her drive past," Tim put in. "I think it was Alex's aunt."

"Yes, Aunty Rhonda," I said. "I saw her, too."

"She made me feel nervous," Peter complained. "She wanted names—the coroner's, and the police officers who were at Alex's apartment last night, and the one who came here, but I couldn't remember any names."

"Did she say why she needed to know?"

"No. But then she wanted the place and date and time for Alex's funeral. I told her we didn't know ourselves yet, except that it would be at St. Cecelia's church."

He reached for his beer. "She didn't stay very long."

"She probably came out because she couldn't get through on the phone," I said, "and I'm sure she is sad and upset about Alex."

"Well, so am I," grumbled Peter. "And I'm not going around worrying people with hard questions." A car turned into our driveway.

"Here's Suzanne," said James, as the dogs started their welcoming chorus.

Suzanne had red eyes and a diminished, almost fragile appearance, but she told us her day hadn't been too bad, once she had heard from Tim. "I went next door to visit with my landlady for a bit, and I used her phone to call my mom," she said. "Mom came up from Victoria and stayed for a long time. I wasn't by myself."

Suzanne had refused to come out to our place, even for the afternoon. "You already had enough to do," she told me as we walked toward the kitchen. "You didn't need anybody extra."

"Have you had supper?" I asked.

"Yes."

"Too bad. I was hoping you would be hungry and that would maybe inspire the guys to eat something, too. None of them want to have a sensible meal."

I handed Suzanne a glass of iced tea and added, "Tim has had nothing but coffee all day, aside from the beer he's drinking now. I hope you can get some food into him because he isn't in a good space." Decoded, this meant Tim would probably want to go out looking for drugs or alcohol or both, as soon as he was away from Mom and Dad.

Then, very unfairly, I added to Suzanne's burden with, "Keep an eye on him if you can. I don't want to lose another son."

For some time, youth suicide had been a serious concern for both of us. We had shared our anxieties the previous fall, when a wave of copycat or 'cluster' suicides happened in our area. Copycat suicides were scary; they often followed the death of somebody well known in the community who had taken his or her own life.

Young people with FASD, already miserable at the funeral of a friend or relative who had committed suicide, heard a pious, "He's happy now. He's gone to a better place," and came to an impulsive, unreasoned conclusion; "I want to be happy in a better place, too," or "I want them to give *me* all this attention." These were the folks who might copy the suicide technique of the relative or friend who had recently died. The central component of the equation, their own personal death, often escaped them.

Neither being depressed nor being suicidal was an essential factor in the suicide of individuals who had an FASD. Some, like

Alex, couldn't understand the whole concept of death. If a favourite movie star could die in a violent western this week and be back in a TV comedy next week, they figured it would be the same for them.

Others, with little understanding of danger, would do anything to please a peer group. Two years ago, one of my friends had lost an adopted daughter when she drove a stolen tractor down a steep hill. Officially, due to surrounding circumstances, this event had been termed a suicide, but Tim and Suzanne said the young people they knew thought her death was the result of a dare.

For Suzanne and me, FASD impulsiveness was the real worry. We knew that Tim's lack of impulse control was far worse than Alex's. Nothing could stop Tim from following through on what seemed, at the time, to be a good idea although in retrospect he could see where he had gone wrong. The opposite was true of Alex. He had always been less impulsive than Tim but, due to his lack of reasoning ability, he was unable to understand that he could possibly have made a mistake.

Suzanne finished her drink and collected her belongings. I gave her Constable Gustafsson's phone number, just in case. If Tim got into any trouble, we could at least count on somebody in authority understanding what it was all about.

Tim was already waiting beside the car, eager to get going. As Suzanne got out her keys, he gave me a quick hug. "Bye, Mom. See you tomorrow. Bye, Dad. G'bye, James. Have a nice honeymoon."

"Thanks," replied James. "Have a nice funeral."

Peter soon announced that he was "due for an early shut eye," and went downstairs. I wanted to check my emails. James said if nobody needed him to do anything, he would open a bag of potato chips and relax in front of the TV for a bit. He had decided to stay with us for the night and had already phoned Elaine to let her know.

"She said to say 'Hi' to you and she'll call tomorrow, before we go to the airport. And she reminded me the Bible Study group is meeting at our place this evening, but Zan will go over to help. After that, she'll go to Liz and Rob's apartment for the night because she doesn't want to stay by herself."

"But what about your packing?" I asked. "Shouldn't you be doing that tonight?"

"No problem." James was comfortably stretched out on his father's favourite chair in front of the television. "I'll have time tomorrow morning."

I settled at my desk and started writing emails to the few people who wouldn't have heard about Alex's death. There was a lot of incoming mail, more than twenty letters of condolence from family and friends who either hadn't been able to reach us by telephone or who found writing easier than talking. They all, with one exception, wrote about Alex—sharing their memories, asking about the funeral, and promising to pray or light candles. The exception was a letter from Sara, my editor. Sara's letter wasn't about Alex; it was about me.

> Dear Ruth,
> Words seem utterly useless at times like these, but I am writing nevertheless to let you know that you are in my thoughts and in my heart.
> I was shocked and saddened to learn at work, this morning, that your beloved Alex took his life last night. I can't even begin to imagine the grief and pain and loss you are experiencing right now. And the unfairness of having to deal with this, after all the other struggles...
> Please know that there are many of us out here (me included!) who care about you, and want to see you through this. Let us know how we can be there for you.
> With deepest sympathy,
> Love, Sara

Sara's email was the first thing that day to reach below my shock and create a little pinprick of something—maybe sadness. I wasn't good at recognizing emotions. To avoid any further development of feelings I quickly shut down the computer. James heard me moving around my office and stuck his nose in.

"Going to bed? Good. It's about time."

The telephone rang. We looked at each other. "I guess it's my turn," I sighed, reaching for the office phone, "but whoever this is, it's way too late to be calling."

"Hello," said a stranger's voice. "Is this Ruth Spencer? This is Bellman's uncle, Sylvester Jack. I called to tell you that Bellman's funeral will be here in Campbell River next Wednesday at Our Lady Queen of Peace, and to let you know that you and your husband are welcome to come."

"But his funeral is going to be in Alderlea," I protested.

"No, it will be in Campbell River and Bellman will be buried with his father on the Tzou'in'quam Reserve. We have put Ocean Funeral Services in charge of all the arrangements." He sounded so firm, so positive. For a moment, it seemed as though Peter and I and all of us had somehow gotten it all wrong.

"This isn't making any sense," I said.

James raised an eyebrow. I signaled to him to listen in on the kitchen phone but before he got there, Uncle Sylvester had hung up.

"What was that all about?" asked James as he came back into the office.

"I can't believe it. That was an uncle from Alex's birth family. He said *they* are planning Alex's funeral."

James didn't look surprised. "I thought something unpleasant might happen; that's why I stayed," he said. "I know some of the young guys from the Tzou'in'quam Reserve. Alex didn't like them much."

"This wasn't a young guy," I said doubtfully. "At least his voice wasn't young."

The phone rang again. This time it was a woman who neither introduced herself nor gave me an opportunity to speak.

"Bellman belongs with his family now," she abruptly informed me. "You aren't in charge of his life anymore."

"I haven't been in charge of his life for years," I replied, but she was gone.

The third call was from Stephanie, one of Alex's birth sisters. I remembered Stephanie as an attractive little girl who had come with her mother to visit Alex during his first years of being fostered. At some point, probably when her mother died, Stephanie had gone to live with her father's family. Meeting again as older teens, she and Alex had developed a nice relationship. Later on, Alex became a proud uncle to Stephanie's twin daughters.

"Hi, Stephanie." I said. She was crying, so I added, "This must be terribly hard for you. I know Alex visited you quite often."

"His name is Bellman," said Stephanie, "and of course he stayed with me. I'm his sister."

"Yes, I know. You and the girls will miss him."

Stephanie stopped crying. "You don't know anything," she declared. "You stole him from us. Why won't you give him back? You had him while he was alive. We want him now that he's dead."

I hung up and stared at James. "That was Alex's birth sister, Stephanie," I said slowly, "and Alex loves her, but he wouldn't have been impressed with that phone call. What do you think we should do?"

"We could ignore it all and go to bed," suggested James.

"Better not. There's the phone again and it's your turn to answer. I don't want to listen to any more misery."

"Then I'll take it in the kitchen," said James.

A few moments later he called, "Hey Mom! It's for you. Somebody called Stanley from Generations. He says they've been phoning him, too."

Perfect! This was exactly the help I needed. Being First Nations himself, Stanley would understand the feelings of Alex's birth family, but he also had a business to run.

"Stanley! Thank goodness it's you," I greeted him. "What the heck is going on?"

"That's what I wanted to ask you," said Stanley. "People from the Tzou'in'quam Reserve in Campbell River have been calling me at home for the last half hour. They're telling me Ocean Funeral Services are in charge of Alex's arrangements."

"Well, they aren't," I said.

"That's what I tried to tell them," said Stanley. "But they won't listen. They are saying they want the body and they're coming to

Alderlea tonight to get it. I'm not sure what I should do."

"Isn't Alex at the hospital? I thought Sherry wasn't going to release him until tomorrow morning."

"Yes, and I told them that. But they still think he's at Generations and they're threatening to break in. They probably won't," he added quickly, "but I'd like to call the RCMP if that's okay with you. I didn't want any police involvement without letting you know."

"Go for it!" I said decisively. "You call the police and warn the hospital and I'll phone the coroner's office and leave a message for Sherry. I'll try to get Constable Gustafsson, too. She said we should keep in touch. And I'm not going to answer any more calls tonight."

But the phone didn't ring again.

Fanning the Flames

Friday started early with a call from the coroner.

"Hi, Ruth. It's Sherry. I got your message. Have you heard anything more from Alex's birth family?"

"Not yet."

"Good," said Sherry. "I don't think they'll be phoning you again; they're calling me now. They were up at the hospital last night, and again this morning, wanting to see Alex, but we won't allow that until all this is sorted out."

"We won't allow it, period. I'm not having a bunch of strangers staring at my son," I said. "It's different if Uncle Edward and Aunty Sandra want to see him, or his grandmother, or Stephanie, or Aunty Loretta and Aunty Rhonda because Peter and I know all those people, and they care about Alex and he likes them. But the rest can forget it."

"You might not have any authority over this, Ruth," Sherry warned me. "The people in Alex's birth family think they have all the power and entitlement from here on in. They think Alex was in your care only as a foster child. They don't believe he was ever adopted. Have you got any proof?"

"Of course we have proof."

As with Kathleen and Tim, we had received the usual form letter of congratulation from the government along with Alex's birth certificate when his adoption was completed.

"That's all anybody got, twenty years ago," I told Sherry.

"Do you know where those papers are? Can you get at them easily?"

"Peter probably has them in his filing cabinet downstairs. Why?"

"I think I'm going to need proof of adoption to convince these people that Alex really is adopted," said Sherry.

"I can't understand why they don't already know. As I told you, we sent out adoption cards. Edward and Sandra must have received theirs. It didn't come back with a 'return to sender' on it."

"Alex's immediate birth family might not be involved in this," said Sherry. "But lots of other people are. Some of them are Residential School survivors…"

"That's not going to help," I put in, thinking of my First Nations friends. Those who had lived at residential schools had memories too painful to discuss. We could talk about anything except our school days.

"…and they see Alex as a child who was torn from his family and 'fostered out.' In their minds, he's a 'stolen child.'"

"Well, it wasn't us who stole him and fostered him out," I said. "They're blaming the wrong people."

"I know," sighed Sherry. "But they're angry, and for them, Alex's funeral is all about white people trying to take away their rights again."

After a little pause, she added, "We are extremely concerned about their harassment of the hospital staff last night, and their threats to steal the body. I have withdrawn Alex's release; he wouldn't be safe at the funeral home."

This news of further trouble caught me right in the pit of my stomach and took me back nine years. *It'll be fine as long as you don't eat,* I told myself.

Sherry asked abruptly, "Ruth? Are you all right?"

"Of course. Where do we go from here?"

The birth family's first meeting had been held the previous day in Campbell River. "That's the meeting for the closest relatives to plan the funeral," Sherry explained. "The second meeting, for the extended family, will be held in Alderlea this morning."

Immediate family always sat together at the second meeting, facing their community. The date, time, and place of the funeral would be announced, and people would be asked to volunteer for various chores and duties, everything from preparing the food to traffic control. Anybody who wanted to speak would have a turn.

There was also the suicide component. Youth suicide was a devastating issue in First Nations communities and the elders often had wisdom and compassion to offer. And in Alex's case, the birth family wanted control of the body. They would be looking at legal ways of obtaining that.

"They'll be busy planning Alex's funeral this morning, and we are going to Generations this afternoon to plan Alex's funeral," I remarked.

"I might see you there, depending on how the morning goes," said Sherry.

Over breakfast, James enlightened his father, in three short sentences, regarding last night's telephone conversations and the demands of Alex's birth family. I was glad James was still with us. My explanation would have been too long and too detailed.

"That was Sherry on the phone," I told Peter. "She thinks we might need proof of Alex's adoption."

"I'll get the papers right after breakfast," Peter decided. "What else do we have to do this morning?"

"I'm leaving in about two minutes." James swallowed the last of his orange juice and pushed back his chair.

"We have to get some clothes from Alex's apartment, and we have to go to the funeral home this afternoon. That's all so far."

"Let's go to Alex's place before the traffic gets bad," Peter suggested. "And shall we pick up Tim on the way?"

"Better give James his hugs first," I said, getting ready for the stretch. This son, nearly a foot taller than his mother, was hard to reach. "Travelling blessings, James, and a huge thank you for all your help last night."

"Be sure to tell Elaine 'Hi' from us," added his father.

It was still early when we drove into town. Passing Tzouhalem Big House, we saw several cars parked beside the large unpainted wooden building and more turning into the parking lot. A few men had gathered at the woodpile behind the Big House; others, standing around the front door, were wearing blackface. This, we realized, was the beginning of the second family meeting.

We collected Tim and went on to Alex's apartment block. Tim introduced us to the building manager, who said, "Oh yes, Mrs. Spencer. I've seen you here before."

Clearly delighted to have somebody new with whom to share, he launched into his story of the gruesome discovery he had made late on Wednesday night. We heard about the complaints he had received; the door he had found locked, the witness he had commandeered from across the hall, their slow entry together into Alex's apartment, his horror at the sight of the body on the floor in the bathroom with the shower rail lying beside it, his call to the RCMP, and his collaring of Alex's cousin when she arrived.

"I made her stay and talk to the police," he told us proudly.

I said, rather faintly, "I'm glad you could help."

Peter gave me an anxious look and interrupted the next bit of the report with a curt, "Let's get going."

Even though we had Alex's key, the building manager led the way upstairs with pauses en route to regale us with more details; the reactions of various of his tenants to a death on the premises. He unlocked Alex's door with a flourish and stepped back for us to enter.

"Coming in?" Peter asked, hoping he wouldn't.

"Oh, no, I'll let you carry on," the building manager said hastily, his stories all told, and his duty done. "Please lock the door when you leave."

The police, coroner, and undertakers had left little evidence of their presence. At first glance, Alex's apartment looked just as it had when I was there last Monday, the same meagre furnishings, the same tidy rooms, a few dirty dishes, including my coffee cup stacked beside the sink. But without Alex, the place seemed horribly cold and empty. I felt like an intruder.

Peter quickly closed the bathroom door.

Alex's favourite pieces of jewellery were lying on the kitchen counter—both his eagle pendant and the tiny silver spoon he always wore on chains around his neck. A heavy silver ring should have been there as well; it had been hanging beside the little spoon ever since Alex's birth father had died. We thought it might have fallen on the bathroom floor. None of us wanted to go and see.

A table in the kitchen nook was set for two with placemats carefully arranged, coffee mugs and spoons laid out, the sugar bowl filled, a small carton of cream turning sour, the coffee pot plugged in and hot. Peter unplugged it.

"Alex had everything ready," he said sadly. "He and his cousin were going to have a cup of coffee together right after the show."

On a counter around the corner, I discovered Alex's well worn white and grey raccoon, her bright blue plastic eyes still shining inside a fluffy black mask. This was the last survivor of Alex's stuffed toys that had lived on his bed the whole time he was growing up.

Picture postcards showing photographs of real wolves covered one wall of the living room. Ceramic wolves with toothy grins, carefully arranged in a circle, held pride of place on the coffee table.

"Hey, look at this," I called. "There's a gap at Council Rock. Some of Alex's wolves are missing." Tim couldn't remember and it was Peter's first visit to this apartment, but I had been there four days before. I knew the biggest grouping of four sweetly smiling wolves, surrounded by ceramic flowers, had vanished.

There was a folded paper tucked under one of the figurines. On it, Alex had written, 'To live life to the fullest you must endure all of life's treasures and keep all those cherished to your heart close to you especially in those times of needs'

Tim headed toward Alex's bedroom. "Do you know what kind of clothes we are supposed to get?"

"Yes, something spiffy. That's what Mary Grace said. You know how Alex likes to dress up. A nice shirt and a tie if we can find them, and maybe his black leather jacket? Alex wears that a lot."

"Suzanne gave him that one. He can't wear it in public anymore," said Tim. "It's got a little rip in the back."

"No one will see the back," I explained. "And we aren't having any viewing. This is just for Alex."

Opening the closet door, Tim pulled out Alex's best white dress shirt, neatly arranged on a hanger, with his favourite Mickey Mouse tie already knotted and tucked under the collar.

"Organized like a white man," exclaimed Tim, pretending surprise. "And here's his pants."

We found Alex's jacket on a hook behind the door and stuffed it, along with his good clothes, into a plastic bag. I added shiny black leather shoes from under the bed and socks from the basket of clean laundry Alex had left against the wall.

"Good," said Peter. "That's it. Let's get out of here."

"Hang on a sec," I said slowly. "Somebody besides us has a key to this place. Those wolves are gone and Alex's ring seems to be missing…I think we should take all of his private papers with us."

There were two big boxes under the bed. Each was about three-quarters full of notes, old calendars, bills and receipts, junk mail, recipes, travel brochures, photos, newspaper clippings, tattered magazines, letters, Christmas and birthday cards, and ancient schoolwork. A quick check around the apartment revealed paper of some sort in every drawer and every cupboard. Both boxes were soon filled to overflowing.

"Are we going to drop all this in the nearest dumpster?" asked Peter.

"Certainly not!" I said firmly. "There are good photos of Kaitlyn in there and some of Alex's writing. I want to go through these boxes before any dumping happens."

"Of course." Peter was at his sarcastic best. "And you have nothing else to do."

For the first twenty-five years of marriage, this kind of remark would have sent me into instant appeasement, but my counselling with Mary Grace was bearing fruit.

"That's right," I agreed. "And of course nothing is more important than Alex."

Tim, for the first time since yesterday morning, managed the beginnings of a smile. "If you two have quite finished," he said politely, "I'll hold the door, and you can each carry a box." It was a perfect imitation of his mother; this had always been my way of dousing any hint of a flare up between siblings. "If you can't play nicely together, then let's see if you can work nicely together." Peter and I meekly picked up the boxes. I smiled at Tim as I went through the doorway but Peter paused to give him a salute. Tim locked the door behind us.

Messages had been left on our answering machine while we were gone. Most were for Tim, but one from the secretary at St. Cecelia's confirmed our use of both church and hall for the following Tuesday, with the funeral at 11:15 a.m. I was glad that something was settled. Having a definite date and time for Alex's funeral felt like having an anchor to cling to in the middle of an unfamiliar sea. Especially now that the sea was afloat with other people's baggage.

Although we had not yet had our official meeting with Father Joe, Peter and I already knew the family's role in the organization of a Roman Catholic funeral. This was the third death in six months for which we would have heavy responsibilities. Last November Peter's and Lucy's sister-in-law, Willie, who lived alone in Alderlea, died suddenly. Lucy, her husband Fons, and Peter and I had planned Willie's funeral with Father Joe; she had been buried from St. Cecelia's. Three months after Willie's death, an elderly family friend passed on following a lengthy illness. Having no relatives apart from one nephew far away in England, she had long ago asked Peter and me to be her executors and to take charge of her funeral and burial arrangements.

For a Roman Catholic Mass of Christian Burial, the family usually provided two scripture readers, several Eucharistic ministers to distribute the blessed bread and wine, a couple for the offertory procession, two women to spread the pall over the casket and six men to be pallbearers. Finding somebody to do the music and the flowers for the church were also our responsibilities. Peter and I already had a list of friends and family we wanted to ask, but now things had become a lot more complicated.

How could I phone special friends, especially friends who lived in other towns, and say, "Please be a Eucharistic Minister (or a reader or a pallbearer) for Alex's funeral," if we weren't going to be allowed to have a funeral? Catholics could only have one funeral mass with all the smells and bells. If it happened in Campbell River, then it couldn't be repeated in Alderlea. In that event, we could only hold a memorial service later on at St. Cecelia's.

Early in the afternoon, Zan called. He was home, back from driving James and Elaine to Victoria International Airport; they were safely on their way to Hawaii. James had shared the bizarre events of the evening before and now Zan asked "Any more calls from Alex's birth family?"

"Not to me," I said thankfully. "The coroner is dealing with them now. She said they are having trouble believing we adopted Alex."

"Interesting," remarked Zan. "Have you been to Alex's apartment or is the family doing that, too?"

"They weren't there this morning," I said. "We picked up a bag of clothes and some shoes for Alex to wear in his casket. The building manager would have told us if anybody else had been around. He's quite a talker."

"What about the funeral?"

"Well, we have a date and a time—next Tuesday at 11:15—but we still don't know if we'll be allowed to have a funeral. If we can have it, we'll need six pallbearers. Tim said he would like to do that for Alex and he'll ask Justin. Alex's friend, Frankie, has already offered. I'm hoping you'll be one, and can you ask Conner?"

"That's only five," Zan pointed out.

"I know. Your best friend and Tim's best friend and Alex's best friend. We won't ask anybody else until we know what's happening."

"I'll check in with Conner," Zan promised. "Is there anything more I can do?"

"Not till you're here. I'm counting on you to go with us to see Father Joe tomorrow afternoon, though."

"Yep. That'll work out," said Zan. "I have supper shifts right through till Monday and then Tuesday and Wednesday off."

"That's perfect."

"Alex's last big show," Zan remarked thoughtfully. "At least he won't be naked. If the funeral is here, are we going to have those little folders with a picture of Alex on the front?"

"Yes, we are," I said. "Grandma wants to pay for them. She asked if there was anything she could do to help."

"Nice of her," approved Zan. "I was thinking for the front you could use Alex's graduation picture. His grad was only seven years ago, and he was a teenager then, at the central part of his life. And a professional photograph will usually copy better than a snapshot."

"That's a wonderful suggestion!"

"I thought so, too," said Zan modestly.

I assumed our conversation was finished, but Zan had something more to offer. "Mom, do you remember when Alex wrote his life story for the FASD group? And you said, 'This is Alex's whole life and it fits on two pages.' I guess two pages is all he's ever going to have."

Psych Ward

The next caller was Sherry. The family meeting at Tzouhalem Big House had paused for a lunch break.

She announced, "This thing is getting big, Ruth."

People had been arriving at the Big House all morning, coming in from all over the Island, from Vancouver and the Fraser Valley, and from as far away as Lillooet and Washington, all keen to help Alex's birth family in their fight for justice. Most of them, according to Sherry, hadn't known of Alex's existence before yesterday, but if they were related to any of Alex's birth great grandmothers, no matter how distant the connection, they had the right to speak in the Big House.

Nothing had been resolved during the second meeting. The Family was still determined to take ownership of Alex's body. They were now discussing the pros and cons of getting a court injunction.

"What's that?" I asked.

Sherry explained. An injunction was an order from the courts designed to stop a person or a group from doing something they wanted to do. In this case, the family wanted to put Alex's funeral and burial on hold until a court decided who had control of his body. Unfortunately, because the courts were horrendously backed up, Alex would have to be kept on ice somewhere in Vancouver for eight months, possibly longer, waiting for the judgment.

"And we certainly don't want that to happen," said Sherry. She had told The Family she would try to bring proof of adoption when the third meeting commenced, late this afternoon. Had Peter found the papers?

"Yes."

"Good. I'll get them when I meet you at Generations. I've promised to present The Family's point of view."

"What about our point of view?"

"I've been presenting that all morning," Sherry said, a little wearily, "and so far nobody has heard me except for a couple of elders."

I already knew, without Sherry telling me, the elders who would understand and accept my place in Alex's life. One was Alex's birth grandmother, with whom he had a good relationship, and the other was his grandmother's sister, Aunty Loretta…

School work had been consistently difficult for Alex. Like his sister, Kathleen, he had to put in extra time at home daily to keep up with the other kids in his class. During the summer holidays, I had all five doing math, spelling, and journaling at least three mornings a week, and we always joined the vacation reading programs at the local library. Alex had worked hard for years.

When he graduated, in 1995, Alex felt that he had finished with work and achieved success. He saw only freedom ahead. The fact that he was now expected to join the labour force somehow escaped him. Peter suggested places where he could leave his resume; I reminded him regularly; his siblings were encouraging but Alex continued to enjoy himself. The summer was waning when Peter finally said, "Alex, you have to get a job and start to earn some money. It's time to either pay board here at home or move out." So Alex moved out.

A friend boarding in a private residence downtown told Alex his landlady had a second room empty and available. Her rent was a lot more than any of Alex's siblings had ever paid at home but for Alex, the call of "Liberty!" was the only thing that registered.

Early in September, another friend took him to the Social Services office and showed him how to get onto Welfare. Once he had money in his pocket, any thoughts of finding employment went right out of his head. He decided it would be fun to go back to school and register for some upgrading courses at Malaspina College. A third friend helped him apply for education funding through Tzouhalem Tribes, and Alex had the world by the tail. But in October there were bills in his mailbox, and friends at the door wanting their loans returned. Alex's financial situation began to get complicated.

Our phone rang very early on a Sunday morning. The caller, Alex's friend who boarded with him, said, "Can you come over to talk about something serious?"

"You'd better tell me now."

"Well, it's not good news. Alex is in the hospital. But he's fine…" he added hastily. "He's on Psych Ward."

"Why?"

"Well, he thought he might be planning to do a suicide attempt."

There weren't any calls from the hospital medical staff letting us know what was happening because Alex was eighteen by then and officially an adult. The Emergency Room doctor, who had no knowledge of Alex's previous medical conditions or his FASD, ordered a strong antidepressant. Copying the behaviours of other psych ward patients, Alex got a lot of mileage out of his 'side effects.' Pretty soon he was busy doing 'counselling' and 'mentoring' all over the ward.

Patients on the psyche ward weren't allowed to wear pyjamas and housecoats; they were expected to get up and dress each morning. It was a rule Alex didn't appreciate. He wandered through the hospital all day long and he wanted everybody who saw him to know that he was officially sick. He got around the rule by going barefoot.

Alex couldn't return to the boarding house after his hospital stay; his ex landlady said she didn't want the responsibility of dealing with another suicide attempt. Not that Alex ever had attempted suicide—he only thought he might—but the thought was enough to give him ten attention filled days on the psych ward, and he loved it. I knew he would always remember how much fun he had there.

By the time he was discharged from the hospital, all his belongings had been moved back home. He was going to stay with us until he found a new place to live.

One of the Tzouhalem elders who worked at Malaspina College, and knew Alex's background, had a talk with him about his living arrangements as soon as he got back to school. She then connected him with his Aunty Loretta—a great aunt on his father's side—and Alex decided to board at Aunty Loretta's big home beside the Nanaimo River.

Peter drove Alex's first load—his desk, his clothes, and the most important item, his sound system—up to Nanaimo. After school the following Monday, when Alex had organized his second load, I did the driving and learned the route to Aunty Loretta's place. Alex wanted me to come in and see his room and meet his new family. I had a cup of tea with Aunty Loretta and her daughter, Aunty Rhonda, while Alex unloaded the car. There were a lot of people living in the house with a nice mix of generations including two little preschool girls. Everybody was friendly.

Alex's aunt didn't ask me anything about his background, or the psych ward, or FASD. Maybe she already had enough information from the elders at his school. Or maybe she felt that an aunt who was actually related knew more than his adoptive mom could know. Or maybe she wanted to start with a clean slate. Or maybe I made her nervous. Or maybe she thought, since Alex was an adult, we should all back off.

I did tell her about the antidepressant drugs Alex's doctor had prescribed for him.

One morning, at the beginning of November, we woke to find a message on the answering machine. It was from Alex's Aunty Rhonda, wondering if Bellman was at home or if we knew where he was.

Before I could deal with that, Aunty Loretta phoned, saying Bellman was not back yet. He had been out all night and they had waited up for him; Aunty Rhonda's phone call to us had been at 1 a.m.

Aunty Loretta had let Alex borrow her car, with clear instructions as to the time of return and the places where he wasn't allowed to take it. He had phoned at 10 p.m. (car curfew) to ask if he could bring back two friends who had no place to go for the night. Aunty Loretta had said "No," and Alex had promised to come straight home, but he didn't show. She needed her car and she was angry as well as worried.

Next, I heard from the police in Nanaimo. Aunty Loretta was in their office asking for help to find Alex and her car. The police wanted me to give them more details about his general habits. They also wanted last names, phone numbers, and addresses of all his friends, but I only knew the first names.

If the officer who questioned me passed on all my answers, then Aunty Loretta learned a lot more about Alex, and about FASD, than she knew before.

I called James, hoping Alex had spent the night with him, but he hadn't. No one answered the phone at Aunty Loretta's place for the rest of the morning. Finally, I tried the police station again to see if anybody there knew anything. They said the matter was out of their hands. Since Alex wasn't a minor, they wouldn't search for him for at least twenty four hours and there were no charges "at this time."

After hearing "no charges," I relaxed. The "missing" hadn't worried me. But I hoped Alex still had a place to live and that his aunt got her board money out of him before this happened.

Aunty Loretta called me again that evening; Alex had come back with the car late in the afternoon. She told him that he had already borrowed it for the last time. Even her own grandchildren were mostly not allowed to touch it, and they were reliable.

Alex had met two girls in town and had either believed or had helped them cook up their story of being cold and wet and kicked out with no place to go. When Aunty Loretta told him, "Sorry, no overnight friends; take them to the police station if they are really homeless," he had decided to rent a motel room for the three of them for the night. As far as Alex was concerned he was helping them—obviously the right thing to do. And he had thoroughly enjoyed himself. Aunty Loretta told me all about the marks on his neck.

The girls were sixteen and seventeen. Their father had been out searching for them all night. He said there was no way they could be either wet or cold; they both had jackets and umbrellas, and he had driven them into town himself.

Aunty Loretta read the riot act to Alex. He told her he didn't know about the laws involving minors in sexual situations and he had forgotten he was an adult.

Two weeks later, there was another call from Aunty Loretta. She said Bellman had a doctor's appointment that morning. (Apparently it should have been the day before, but Alex didn't tell anybody he needed a ride until all the cars were booked up.) Aunty Loretta was worried about a lot of things and wanted me to phone the doctor as she understood he was my doctor, too.

She asked me how much Bellman had been drinking at home.

"Nothing!"

Well, she had been down to collect his laundry and had found five big bottles of hard liquor in his room, all started. He had rum and two kinds of scotch and vodka and something bright blue that she couldn't identify. She said, "We don't drink at our place, except for the occasional beer on a hot day."

Also, Aunty Rhonda had dropped Alex off at the college and had then remembered something she needed to get from him and had gone back, but he had already vanished—she thought into the pub. Aunty Loretta was afraid that Prozac and booze were a bad combination and she felt the doctor should know.

I wished I didn't know.

Aunty Loretta told me the counsellors at the college were *only* school counsellors. She thought Bellman needed a psychiatrist or a psychologist and Dr. Smith should do a referral for him to get his behaviour straightened out. I promised to phone the doctor and pass on her message. I also said it would be a good idea if whoever drove Alex to the doctor's office actually went in with him to see the doctor. I said, "Dr. Smith is used to that, and so is Alex. He often needs help understanding directions and remembering what was said."

That turned out to be the right thing for me to say. Aunty Loretta finally began to ask me some questions about things like maturity, mood swings, poor appetite, Bellman's lack of studying after his First Nations Band had funded his courses, and her having to remind him to take a shower and clean his teeth.

"I'm not prepared to be a babysitter," she said.

The next caller was Alex, wanting me to meet him at the college. He said he needed to put in some grievances about his new family who, he claimed, didn't understand him.

"They try to get me to eat and I don't want to eat."

Aunty Loretta already knew Alex had always been thin, but maybe she didn't realize that this poor management of hunger was part of his FASD rather than a protest against her cooking. Anyway, Alex looked pretty good to me, and I thought they were doing fine in the kitchen department.

"If you want the scolding to stop," I said, "you'll have to eat *something* at mealtimes. Just take a teensy bit of everything. That's what I have to do."

"I do that but then they give me more," Alex protested.

"Well, that's a waste. I hope they have dogs or chickens."

"And they always want me to talk, and I have nothing to say."

I sighed. "This is a cultural issue, Alex. You'll have to explain that you come from a family that doesn't talk incessantly. Well, except for Kathleen; she always has a lot to share. But the rest of us don't chatter—we only say what we need to say."

Alex remembered we had discussed this once before and he thought he could make Aunty Loretta understand.

"They think I don't dress warmly enough. Aunty Loretta went and bought me a new jacket and some other things."

New clothes didn't sound like a problem to me. We should all be so lucky! But Alex, with three older brothers passing garments down the line, already had his full quota of good jackets and nice sweaters and warm underwear. If he chose not to dress for the weather, then let him be cold. That was my opinion.

His main complaint was the lack of freedom to choose his own walking place and time.

"I go out alone at night and they don't like that, especially not if I go past the graveyard. I'm not supposed to eat outside at night either. They say the spirits don't like it. They tell me where I shouldn't go and they say when I have to be back."

"That part is not new," I said. "Dad and I always wanted to know where you were going. If a person goes out alone at night and breaks his ankle and can't get home, how will anybody know where to search if he hasn't said where he will be?"

"But it was different at home."

"Yes. But that was because I always said, 'When do you plan to be back?' and, 'Can you give me an idea of where you'll be?' I don't like telling other people what they should do."

"However!" I added, making Alex laugh, "Why don't *you* say those things before anybody asks? When you leave, do an announcement: 'I'm going out for a walk to the river—or wherever—and I'll be back in an hour.' Then you are the one in charge of what you do."

Five days before the end of November Alex phoned, being charming. He wanted me to co-sign for a loan. I said, "No," so he wanted to talk to Dad.

Peter said, "He doesn't usually want to talk to me. What's it all about? Money?"

Alex was out of luck. He wasn't pleased with either of us and we heard nothing more from him for a few days. Then, on the first of December, Aunty Loretta phoned to tell us Alex was back in the hospital: it was officially a suicide attempt.

She said Alex had written great stacks of pages about suicide and death and how he was "going to do it." As usual, nothing was checked over after he wrote it. Aunty Loretta said words were missing, punctuation was missing, the spelling was unusual, and it was hard to follow his ideas.

Then, a couple of days before his planned event, he gave Aunty Loretta a suicide note. She didn't take it very seriously; she thought since no one would co-sign for the loan he wanted, he was annoyed and getting even. She was pretty fed up with him.

I didn't think it was that simple, but I also didn't think Alex was suicidal. Aunty Loretta and I agreed—taking a handful of pills and then giving two of his housemates the empty packages, as Alex had done, was an attention grab, not a suicide attempt.

Alex phoned Aunty Rhonda from the hospital late one night, after she had gone to bed, being unbelievably demanding about his bank card. He wanted it "right now!" He said he had to sign himself out of the hospital and go to a motel; he had to be alone.

Aunty Rhonda called me the next morning to ask me what she should do.

"Don't let him have his bank card," I said, promising to inform Dr. Smith and Alex's psychiatrist, Dr. Jacques, immediately. To my surprise, both doctors asked to see me right away.

Talking to Dr. Jacques in person was difficult. She couldn't say very much because of patient confidentiality, and I couldn't say very much because she was a stranger. But one of us had to talk, for Alex to get the help he needed, so I said my bit with difficulty, wishing Mary Grace could have been there, too. For me, it was a scary half hour, even though Dr. Jacques said our conversation had answered many of the question marks on Alex's file.

At the end of our time together, when all the hard topics had been covered, and I was feeling like a floppy stalk of celery too long at the back of the fridge, Dr. Jacques did a most amazing thing: she asked what I wanted for Alex. A specialist actually caring about the mother's opinion was almost unheard of in FASD circles.

"That's easy! I want what Alex needs the most—structure, lots of support, and permanent supervision. But don't worry," I added, seeing her face change. "I know none of those are going to happen."

Dr. Smith, our family doctor, said he wanted to keep Alex in for another week, and even refused to write a pass allowing him to come home for an evening to celebrate St. Nicholaas Day.

"Alex's housing might become an issue again," I told Dr. Smith. For one thing, Aunty Loretta wanted him to have counselling before he went back to her place. For another, Alex was now thinking in terms of his own apartment because "Those people are driving me nuts."

I went to the hospital every day that week although some days it was hard to visit Alex. He said he didn't want to go back to Aunty Loretta because she interfered in his life. (He used to say that about Mom and Dad, too. What he really wanted was total freedom along with total support.)

He said he didn't want to stay in the hospital. (But we knew he loved the place.)

He said he wanted to switch to Camosun College because the Malaspina College staff wouldn't let him take the courses he felt qualified to take. (Never mind how badly his assessments had turned out, or the fact that he had already failed his first course, or his many skipped classes. Those were minor details. *Feeling qualified* was what counted.)

Anybody who disagreed with him was "arguing." In fact, everybody was wrong about everything, except for Alex. When I visited, he was usually either enormously sorry for himself or almost boiling over with anger. Sometimes he was so verbally abusive I left before visiting hours were over. My problem was I could only love him—I couldn't help him.

At the end of the week, Dr. Smith phoned to give me what he called "a heads up." He had told Alex he was ready to be discharged. Alex had refused to leave the hospital and had suddenly become enormously teary and depressed. He assured Dr. Smith he would be back in the hospital in the same condition in forty-eight hours if he was sent home before he was ready to go.

Dr. Smith left it up to Dr. Jacques, who said Alex could have two more days if he worked on a behaviour contract. But, said Dr. Smith, according to the staff on the psych ward, the minute the doctors were gone and Alex had got his own way his 'depression' lifted and he was back on the phone, laughing and chatting with his friends.

That afternoon, I drove Alex to Aunty Loretta's place so he could get more clothes and some music for the next two days. He planned to take these back to his hospital room; then he would sign himself out again and I was to drive him on into town where he could do some shopping.

Aunty Loretta hadn't seen Alex since he had disrupted the family with his latest suicide attempt. She had a lot to say, and we both had to listen to the lecture but Alex didn't pay attention. When she had barely finished speaking he asked her for his wallet—but his Aunty Rhonda had it and she wasn't there. A disgruntled Alex went to pack up his tapes and clothes, while I had a soothing cup of tea and a peaceful visit with Aunty Loretta.

Renske Vandersluys, Alex's nurse (and my favourite nurse when I was living on the psych ward for nine weeks the year before) was waiting for us when we got back to the hospital. She said she needed to talk to Alex about his behaviour contract and she wanted me to be there, too; she said all I had to do was listen. I hoped neither of them realized how unnerving that was for me, even though this was Alex's problem, not mine.

Alex was supposed to be spending his last two days in hospital working on a list of things that would be a help in stopping his next suicide attempt from happening: the names of people he could phone if he felt suicidal, somebody he could put in charge of his pills, and any effort he was willing to make toward getting some counselling. He had been told to have it written up and signed by that evening. But Alex said he hadn't started it yet. He was very casual and obviously not the least bit interested.

I said, "Well, I won't be driving you into town if you haven't done your homework."

Renske quickly agreed and she put us into the conference room to have a little chat. Our chat lasted three seconds.

I said, "Nope," to the pleading look and Alex said, "I'll get some paper." He had his contract written and signed in seven minutes.

Alex didn't need me to drive him into town; it wasn't far and he could have walked perfectly well. He was allowed to sign himself out of the hospital between meals, and his nurse wanted him to get more exercise. This was one of the few times his lack of reasoning ability worked in my favour.

While he did his writing I told Renske I was glad she was the nurse on duty because it was nice to hear a bit of her wisdom again, especially when it was being directed at somebody else.

But there was something I wish I hadn't noticed. When we were both with Renske, Alex was sitting up straight, with his feet on the floor and his hands on the chair arms. I was sitting nervously scrunched, with my feet tucked up on the chair, and my hands twisted and clenched. And even after I became aware, I couldn't straighten out.

After Alex finished his contract, he signed himself out of the hospital for two hours. I dropped him off in town, expecting him to do his bit of shopping and walk back but Alex expected to spend the night in a motel. Unfortunately for him, he couldn't. He had a nasty surprise at the bank. When he had phoned Aunty Rhonda the week before, demanding his bank card and "needing to be alone," she had emptied his account for his own protection.

Alex, in a steaming temper, called the police with a charge of theft against his aunt. The police phoned Aunty Rhonda, who told them about Alex being a patient on the psychiatric ward. She said she had put his money in a safe place and could prove it hadn't been stolen or used. Then she called me to share Alex's latest. She also called Nurse Renske.

Renske promptly organized a meeting for the next day between Alex and herself and the aunts. Alex had a few moments of regular visiting time with me beforehand, which he spent clinging to my arm and crying. He told me Aunty Rhonda had taken his money— (but he said nothing about his call to the police.)

I said, "Alex, that is the best help you could ever have. You can see for yourself that all your money vanishes in a week. By the end of the month, you are always broke and suicidal."

Alex was unimpressed.

We heard Renske's shoes coming down the hall, and I got ready to leave so the others could have their meeting. But Renske wanted a word with Alex before he joined his aunts and she wanted me to stay and listen to that word.

Alex had written in his contract that his aunts would handle his meds for him, but he hadn't bothered to ask his aunts. When Renske mentioned it to them, they didn't know what she was talking about. They said they definitely didn't want that kind of responsibility. But they did want Alex to respect the family curfew on school nights and to refrain from running up any more long distance telephone bills. And they didn't want him bringing booze into the house. Alex said nothing, and Renske said, "Ruth? Those are your rules too, aren't they?"

I said, "Yes."

Renske asked me if I wanted to join the meeting. I didn't, but I should have anyway because, once there, Alex refused to cooperate. When he phoned later, very annoyed with me, he said, "It was three against one, so I didn't talk and Renske gave me a lecture afterwards. I've had lectures from everybody today," and "I'm going to leave Aunty Loretta's and share an apartment with Molly."

Molly was the cute little sixteen year old who had been in the psych ward for a few days the week before. They'd been phoning each other, every hour on the hour, ever since she went home.

Tuesday, December 13 was a difficult day, starting with an unpleasant call from the ward clerk on Psyche. Alex had engineered another suicide attempt the evening before. This time he used pills I had helped him get hold of; he had hidden them in his backpack when I took him to Aunty Loretta's place for more clothes. The receptionist wanted to know if I could come in on Friday morning for a meeting about Alex. Dr. Jacques would be there, and the aunts, and Alex's psychiatric ward nurses, and the hospital social worker, and somebody from Drug and Alcohol.

Later in the day, Aunty Loretta phoned. She had also received a call from the hospital about Friday's meeting and she wanted us to pool our information. She didn't want either of us to get any more disagreeable surprises. We discussed Alex's latest suicide attempt, knowing it had been staged to prevent his doctors from discharging him. I told Aunty Loretta about the cute little sixteen year old Alex had met last week, who was now his choice of roommate.

Aunty Rhonda and Aunty Loretta, I noticed, had both stopped calling Alex "Bellman."

That day was a Christmas baking day for me with no time to visit at the hospital until after supper. When I finally got there, Alex was being a smart aleck and too big for his britches, and his nurse didn't leave his room. Although I already knew the answer, I asked him why he hadn't been discharged.

Alex said, "I ate a lot of pills and then I told my nurse right afterwards."

I asked, "Why did you eat them?" knowing he understood the

connection between taking the pills and not being discharged, but Alex answered, "Well, I knew fourteen wouldn't kill me because twenty one hadn't."

"So why tell the nurse?" I inquired. "Why tell anyone if the pills weren't going to kill you anyway?"

As usual, when any reasoning was asked for, Alex couldn't handle it. He got mad instead.

"This visit is over," he informed me. "I haven't got anything else to say."

We all came together on Friday morning and had our big meeting about Alex: Aunty Loretta and me, Dr. Jacques, Carla and Phil Chong, who were two of the psych ward nurses I remembered from my own time in hospital, and Sadie from Drug and Alcohol Counselling. The hospital social worker couldn't come. Nobody introduced anybody and Sadie said to me, "Are you Alex's foster mother or something?"

"I'm his mother," I answered.

Sadie gave Aunty Loretta a confused look and Dr. Jacques explained, "This is Alex's aunt."

I said, smiling at Aunty Loretta, "Aunty Loretta is actually related to Alex. I'm not."

"There are lots of ways to be related," said Dr. Jacques.

Aunty Loretta was definitely on my side; she kept on telling the group how hard this whole thing was for Alex's mother. She said, "I've heard a lot about these FASD kids, but I've never had to live with one till now and six weeks is enough for me!" She had already decided that she didn't want to have him back.

We were there all morning—it turned into a mini workshop on severe FASD brain damage. Phil was the most interested and kept asking questions that had nothing to do with Alex.

I said, "You're learning a lot, aren't you, Phil?" and he said, "Yes! I'm really glad you came."

Aunty Loretta talked about Alex's belongings. I said Peter and I would have to retrieve them because Alex never would, and she said there wasn't much.

"I know," I said, having already gained a lot of previous experience. "When our kinds of kids grow up they don't own very much because they can't keep track of their things by themselves. Whenever they move or get evicted they leave most of their stuff behind. And they usually don't have any hobbies or any particular interests, apart from self and survival." That was hard for Phil to understand. He told us he has piles of hobbies and not enough time for them all.

Aunty Loretta said, "Has anybody thought about the Moffatt Clinic for Alex?"

Dr. Jacques explained, in complicated medical jargon, all the reasons why that wouldn't be appropriate, but all Aunty Loretta understood was that Alex was too old for the Moffatt Clinic programs. (And thank God he *was* too old; their approach, at that time, was *not* geared to FASD.) My opinion must have shown; Dr. Jacques asked if I had anything to add.

I said, "Their programs are for kids with behaviour problems. Being exposed to Behaviour Management wouldn't do anything for Alex. His problem is permanent brain damage and he needs permanent support and supervision because he can't change."

Dr. Jacques asked for my opinion regarding counselling for Alex.

I said, "Even if he managed to get himself to all the sessions, I don't think twelve sessions in twelve weeks is going to do any good for somebody who needs direction every half hour. And I also question the value of counselling for a kid with no reasoning ability."

The doctor agreed with me right away on that one; she had been trying to reason with Alex for the last ten days and getting no place.

Dr. Jacques brought up Alex's latest 'attempt' and the fact that he had picked up the pills he used during a visit home. Aunty Loretta had a lot to say about that, and she finished off with telling us how much anger she felt at Alex. And nobody said anything.

Dr. Jacques said, "Ruth?"

I said, "I feel sick with guilt because I never thought to check his back pack," and they all jumped on me with, "You mustn't feel that way!" That was the only thing Carla said through the whole meeting.

I couldn't understand why it was appropriate for Aunty Loretta to have feelings but not appropriate for me to have them. Nor why was it acceptable to feel angry but not acceptable to feel guilty. Mary Grace always told me, "Feelings aren't right or wrong; they just are. Own your feelings!"

The meeting was supposed to be about finding housing for Alex but in the end, they dumped that onto the hospital social worker who wasn't even there. If she expected Alex to take on any responsibility in that area, she would be sadly disappointed. He didn't want to be housed; he wanted to be hospitalized.

Smouldering

By the time we were ready to leave for the funeral home, I was worn out. Memories, missed meals, lack of sleep, and anxieties regarding Tim's mental state and Alex's birth family were all starting to catch up with me. Peter was tired, too. We automatically took our usual route into town, forgetting that we would have to pass the Tzouhalem Big House again.

Sherry had been right; the family meeting *was* getting big. Cars filled the parking lot and overflowed, double-parked, far up and down the road. We noticed with relief that there weren't very many people about and assumed the lunch break was over and all were back inside.

But our little City of Alderlea was busy, even for a Friday. As we crested Memorial Hill and turned right onto Preston Street, I vaguely noted a large group running across the road below the next intersection. Police cars were parked at either end of Preston.

Stanley, the funeral director, met us at Generations' front door. Dispensing with his usual formal greeting, he asked abruptly, "Where did you park?"

"Right beside your building." Peter pointed to our truck. "Is that the wrong place? I can move it."

"No, leave it right there. The police will be able to keep an eye on it," said Stanley. "Alex's family are all over the place," he added as he led us inside. "They are preventing me from doing my job."

I handed over Alex's graduation picture, my obituary, which was finished with the now tentative funeral date and time, and the bag of clothes Stanley had asked for. He looked gloomily at the clothes.

"Let's hope this gets sorted out soon," he said.

Peter went on through the hallway with Stanley, listening to his complaints, but I turned back to greet Suzanne and Tim who had come in right behind us. Tim looked curled in on himself like a dandelion sprayed with weed killer. Suzanne seemed awkward and uncomfortable.

"I hope you don't mind that I came, too," she said anxiously.

"Are you kidding? I was expecting you. Actually, I don't think I could manage this without you."

Suzanne smiled and hugged me. "Yes, you could," she said. "You're keeping us all going." She reached back and caught Tim's hand. "Tim, tell your mom about Justin."

"I phoned him," mumbled Tim. Always soft spoken, today his voice was little more than a whisper. "He can't be a pallbearer for Alex."

I leaned closer, trying to hear. "Why not?"

"He has to go to jail that day."

"Is he sure?" I asked.

"Yes. He has a court date for next Tuesday morning and he's pleading guilty. The lawyer already told him he'll have to do some time."

"Does the lawyer know about Alex?" I asked.

Tim shrugged. "I never told him."

Justin and Tim both used the services of Thao Tran, who was, in my opinion, Alderlea's best and most empathetic criminal lawyer. Thao's caseload included a more or less permanent clientele of repeat offenders, most of whom qualified for government legal aid. He got paid for maybe a quarter of the time he spent with each of his Legal Aid clients.

Peter knew Thao through the pottery courses his wife taught in her home studio. Thao liked to wander through the workroom admiring the creations of his wife's students. Peter was one of the students. I kept in touch with Thao through FASD circles as well as through Tim's frequent difficulties with the law.

"I'll call Thao's office as soon as we finish here," I promised. "He might be able to get the trial put forward to Tuesday afternoon. Then Justin could at least come to the funeral. He'd probably be too stressed to be a pallbearer, though."

Tim nodded. "He wants to come. Thanks, Mom."

"Ruth?" Peter was standing behind me. "Stanley would like us to choose a casket before the other people get here."

"What other people?"

"Some of Alex's birth family thought they could come and plan the funeral with us." Feeling my sudden tension he added, "Don't worry. Stanley said 'No,' but he told them they could send someone to represent them. So they're sending the coroner and some police officers."

"I already knew about Sherry coming," I said, "but police? That's not going to be very good for Tim…or for me either. Why do we need *them*?"

"Having the police here is the best way to keep The Family from coming in and disrupting us," affirmed Stanley.

"Will it be Constable Gustafsson?" I asked, thinking to myself, *a good choice for me—a bad choice for Tim.*

"I don't know who they'll send," said Stanley as he smoothly ushered us through another door.

In this room there were three layers of caskets on shelves around the walls, with a few cremation boxes standing upright in corners. Casket colours, except for the polished hardwoods, were uniformly dull. Some lids were closed but for most the top half had been left open showing inside linings of white satin and lace. Alex was not a satin and lace sort of person. I looked around for something navy blue and masculine.

"This is what the government provides for people on income assistance," said Stanley, pointing to a closed casket on the middle shelf closest to the door. It was light grey, smoothly finished, nicely curved, and solid looking, with three silver handles on each side and no other ornamentation. It was perfect; I knew Alex would have liked it.

"Yes, that's fine," said Peter.

Next, Stanley showed us some memorial books. "You might like to have one for your records," he said. "There are pages for relatives and friends to sign at the funeral."

I wasn't keen. The books were loose leaf and off-size; getting more paper would be a challenge. They were also expensive. But Peter was wiser than me. He knew that I would want to save every scrap of information connected to Alex and quickly realized that the memorial book would make that task much easier. He had also caught Tim's expression.

"Which one do you like, Tim?" he asked.

"That one," said Tim quickly, pointing to a bald eagle soaring over a heavy fir forest. I was glad the decision had been taken out of my hands.

Stanley wrote something in his ever present notebook and directed us into the meeting room. Sherry was already there. When we had settled ourselves, Suzanne and Tim were at the end of the table, Sherry, Peter and I were on one side, and Stanley was sitting with his back to the door. There were two empty chairs directly across the table from me, waiting for the police officers. The seating seemed almost to have been planned in advance. I was tempted to move around beside Suzanne to see what would happen.

Peter handed Sherry Alex's adoption papers.

"Thanks. This should help," she said, putting the envelope carefully into her briefcase. "While we're waiting, I'll tell you what's happening over at the Big House."

In BC, the law provides an Order of Authority, Sherry told us, which lays out very clearly who has the legal right to be in charge of anybody's final disposition. In Alex's case, with no will, no spouse, no adult children or grandchildren, and, as they believed, no adoption, The Family had expected control of Alex's body to go to Stephanie, his adult sibling. Because these expectations were being threatened, The Family had decided to use the courts to get what they wanted. Obtaining a court injunction was the first step.

Parents are listed before siblings in the Order of Authority. With our proof of parenthood, there was no doubt Peter and I would win in a court of law. Eventually. And while we were all waiting for our day in court, Alex would be stretched out on ice somewhere waiting to be buried. My thoughts kept skittering away from this idea, and I wondered how his birth family could bear to hold it in the front of their minds.

Sherry looked around the table. "If you people could come to some compromises with your funeral and burial arrangements that The Family could accept," she suggested, "they might be willing to forget about this court action."

She glanced down at her notes. "One of the problems will be that they want to have a full body burial."

"We want cremation," Peter put in.

"But if a full body burial will make the birth family more peaceful," I said slowly, "I guess it wouldn't devastate us." Peter looked irritated but said nothing.

"I'll need the body for embalming," reminded Stanley, "and that can't wait much longer."

"Another problem," Sherry went on, "is that The Family wants Alex to be buried beside his father at the Tzou'in'quam Cemetery in Campbell River…"

"But we might not be allowed to visit his grave if it's on reserve," I objected, "and anyway, we want him here in Alderlea, at St. Matthew's, where most of my ancient ancestors are buried. We used to go there for Sunday walks when our kids were little, so it's familiar territory."

"…And they want a ceremonial funeral and burial with all the native rites and traditions," finished Sherry.

In the silence that followed, we heard the outer door close and footsteps in the hallway—the police had arrived. Tim tensed visibly and clutched Suzanne's hand. The meeting room doorway filled overwhelmingly with black and yellow uniforms…

…and then Peter smiled and I took a deep, calming breath and Tim relaxed, leaning back in his chair—because these officers were friends.

Peter already knew Kelly, who did public relations for the Alderlea RCMP detachment and was police liaison to the local Speed Watch group. Peter volunteered for Speed Watch and had worked with

Kelly several times over the last two years, monitoring highway traffic. He stood to shake her hand.

And Tim and I already knew Greg, a big First Nations RCMP officer. Deeply involved with interventions for adults with FASD before he had been assigned to Alderlea, he had joined the Prevost Valley FASD Action Team Society soon after he arrived here. Greg and I were both society board members. I hopped up, miraculously without tripping over any furniture, and shared a hug with him.

Neither Kelly nor Greg had ever arrested Tim although both were aware of his police record. In a small town, the repeat offenders were hard to miss. But Greg's acquaintance with Tim was through the heavy labour he occasionally took on for the FASD Action Team, and not through the legal system.

The atmosphere in the room lightened.

"Before we get started, there's a big question out there regarding family rights," said Greg. "The Jacks are saying Alex was never adopted. Is that correct?"

"Alex is adopted," I said firmly, "and Sherry has the papers to prove it."

But even with proof of adoption, Sherry told us, there were members of Alex's birth family who were going to insist on a court injunction. The trouble wasn't coming from the whole family but from a small political group, most of whom never even knew Alex. But they were loud and persuasive and they were fighting for the rights of all First Nations everywhere.

"We can't change that," said Sherry. "We're here to try to work out a compromise with the rest of The Family so Alex can have a funeral this week and not eight months down the road."

"These are the things that have to be decided," said Stanley, quickly flipping through pages. "The Spencers want the funeral to be in Alderlea, at St. Cecelia's church, with cremation to follow and they want to bury Alex's ashes here in town. The Jack's want the funeral to be in Campbell River at Our Lady Queen of Peace and they want Alex to be buried on Tzou'in'quam Reserve beside his father."

"They want full body burial and a viewing," Greg interrupted.

"And the Spencers don't want any viewing," concluded Stanley.

"However, they are willing to consider full burial. What about the natives—are they willing to bend on any point?"

Sherry shook her head. "I don't think so."

"There is one thing nobody has mentioned," I said slowly, searching for the right words. "Alex's birth mother was buried here in Alderlea; she's in St. Paul's graveyard out on Bruton Road. Alex visited her grave often. I'm not sure exactly which bit of the graveyard she's in, or if there is any room round about… Do you think The Family would be willing to have Alex buried beside his mother instead of his father?"

"I can ask them," said Sherry. "It's a very good idea."

"What about a viewing?" asked Greg. "That's really important to the First Nations folks. The immediate family still hasn't been allowed to see Alex at the hospital."

"That's because there have been threats from some of the other people to steal his body," said Sherry. "I'm taking those threats very seriously, and so are the hospital authorities."

"The funeral is tentatively planned for Tuesday morning at Saint Cecelia's. They could have their viewing here at Generations chapel beforehand if that's all right with the Spencers," said Stanley. "Are you folks comfortable with having a viewing here?"

"I'm not," flatly from Peter.

"We have already talked about this. Peter and I don't want any viewing at all," I said. "But Tim doesn't mind, so if it's all right with Peter, maybe Tim can make the final decision?" Peter nodded reluctantly. "And if Tim agrees, would he and his friends be allowed to view as well?"

"Of course," said Stanley.

"Then I guess it's okay," said Tim. "As long as I can keep an eye on those Indians."

Stanley turned to a new page in his notebook. "They can have their viewing at 9 on Tuesday morning for an hour," he said, "but that's all they're getting. There won't be any more time. We'll be taking Alex to the church at 10:15 a.m."

"We want a closed casket at the church," I reminded him.

Sherry was checking her notes. "Alex has a sister in Kimberly and a brother in Hawaii. They can't be at the funeral," she told Greg and Kelly, "and that's why his mom and dad wanted cremation now and a small service at the cemetery for the family later on."

"The birth family will want a big traditional burial ceremony right after the funeral," said Greg.

"I take it both families are Catholic?" Kelly asked. There were nods around the table. "And isn't St. Paul's a First Nations Catholic church?" More nods. "So if the birth family agreed to a burial there, wouldn't they automatically be getting a traditional ceremony?"

Stanley and Greg looked at each other. Both brown First Nations faces looked uncertain. "They would be getting a Tzouhalem ceremony," said Stanley reluctantly.

"Aren't most of them Tzouhalem?" asked Kelly.

"No," said Greg. "Most of the people I've talked to belong to the Tzou'in'quam Band. That's up near Campbell River."

"But they're meeting here."

"Only because Alex is in Alderlea," explained Sherry. "If he had died in Campbell River, these big meetings about him would have been held there. But I think St. Paul's church authorities and the Tzouhalem elders could cope very well with something like this if The Family will agree to it."

"What about our family?" I asked. "Would we be allowed to go to the graveyard?"

"I don't know," said Sherry. "It's one of the things we'll be sorting out at the third meeting. Hopefully, there will be some answers for all of us by tonight."

"And hopefully I'll get the body," grumbled Stanley. "I need to be able to get on with my job. Those natives are preventing me from doing my work," he added for the benefit of Kelly and Greg.

"I'll release Alex as soon as I can," Sherry promised patiently.

"And we'll try to keep the peace," said Kelly, smiling at Peter as she and Greg moved toward the door.

Sherry glanced at her watch. "The next family meeting will be starting soon," she said, "but before I go and listen to them, I'd like to hear a bit more from Alex's real family. All this extra stress must be terribly hard for you."

"It is," growled Peter. "I'm getting tired of it. We're not getting anything we want. We want cremation and no viewing and we're getting a viewing and no cremation. And it sounds like we can't even bury Alex at St. Matthew's."

"At least he might be in Alderlea," I observed.

"You folks are being incredibly generous," said Sherry softly. "How are you doing, Ruth?"

"I'm all right. But I'm wondering if there's any point planning for a funeral that might never happen."

"I think you should go ahead and plan," Sherry was definite. "The Family will need more time, but I think they will accept these changes in the end. I'll phone you tonight," she added as she left.

Stanley, ready with his notebook, quickly took the rest of us through Generations' responsibilities for the next few days, which appeared to be mainly transporting Alex from the hospital morgue to the funeral home, from the funeral home to the church, then probably from the church to the cemetery rather than the crematorium. He had been in touch with Alex's worker at Income Assistance; all the clerical, transportation, storage, and disposal costs would be covered.

Would we be planning the funeral with Father Joe on Saturday? Stanley was already familiar with Father Joe's way of doing things; they could sort out any issues between themselves.

He had the obit, and would get it into the Wednesday papers, "… after the funeral, unfortunately."

He had the picture of Alex and would order two hundred service folders immediately. Generations would provide the vital stats for page three. We could choose a poem or a Bible reading for page two. He offered a big binder of possible choices.

"Maybe it would be better to use some of Alex's writing instead," I suggested, "if that's okay with Tim and Peter. What about the page we found on his coffee table under the wolf?" They both agreed. I took it out of my pocket and handed it to Stanley.

"I want it back," I said firmly." The original, not a copy."

"You'll get it," Stanley assured me, clipping note and photograph together.

"Now there's something else I want you all to be aware of—nothing to do with us, but it's usually part of a native burial. The birth family will probably purchase a vault." Seeing our blank looks, he told us a vault was an outer burial container with a curved lid. The dirt was piled up over it, giving the grave a high, rounded look that would last for a couple of years until time and the weather flattened it.

"Vaults are provided by the cemetery," Stanley finished. "That's why they're not part of our services."

Sherry had signed the medical certification, and Stanley had already registered the death. He would call us as soon as Alex's death certificate crossed his desk and we could come in and pick it up.

"And one more thing," Stanley steepled his hands and looked at us across his fingertips. "Can you bring in some of Alex's clothes?"

"They're already here," I reminded him. "You put the bag behind your desk."

"Those are good clothes for dressing Alex and making him look nice for the viewing if we have it. Those are the clothes he will be buried in," Stanley explained carefully. "The natives will want another set of everyday clothes for the Burning."

"The what?"

"The Burning. It's traditional," said Stanley quickly. "First the funeral, then the burial rites at the cemetery, then they'll all go back to the Big House for the Burning. In the old days, they burned everything the dead person owned, but now the only thing they'll want from you is a bag of clothes."

"Too bad," said Tim crossly, and Peter looked equally uncooperative. Stepping into the breach for the third time, I said, "If we did agree to do this, the only clothes they would get would be worn out. We want to keep a few things ourselves and everything else that's decent is going down to the Salvation Army or Bibles for Missions. There's no way we would waste perfectly good clothes in a fire."

"That's fine," said Stanley, looking relieved. "They'll want clothes and shoes that Alex has actually worn. It doesn't matter what condition they're in."

I stood up, more than ready to leave but surprising myself with

Smouldering

this abruptness. My usual way was to wait until the authority, in this case Stanley, closed the meeting and to let Peter lead the goodbyes.

Memories

Since Sherry had said we should go ahead with our funeral planning, the rest of my afternoon was spent on the telephone. Long explanations were necessary. I was inviting friends and family members to be part of an event that we hoped would be a Roman Catholic funeral mass but could become a memorial service or might even have to be postponed indefinitely. Even so, I found this series of calls asking for help at Alex's funeral a lot more pleasant than yesterday's calls, telling everybody he had died. Today, with the first shock over, people had stories to tell and memories to share.

My brother Bruce, having agreed to be a pallbearer, said, "I was trying to remember the last time I talked to Alex. It must have been late Wednesday morning, maybe about ten hours before he died."

Bruce had been driving one of the Muni trucks that day—he worked for the Municipality of North Prevost—and Alex saw him pulling up at a stop sign. He ran across the street to say "Hi, Uncle Bruce!" the same as always.

"You know Alex, always watching every driver. He never missed a friend," Bruce said. "He sure wasn't depressed when I saw him."

Vera was a longtime supporter of our family. She was older than us and no longer in the best of health. When Peter and I married and became members of St. Cecelia's parish, Vera was one of the people we got to know right away. Her interests paralleled ours, even though her children were already into their teens and we hadn't started a family yet. We met her at many church meetings and social events.

My three youngest started their Roman Catholic religious education lessons (similar to the Protestant Sunday School but taught at home in those days) with Vera as their program corrector. The boys' completed papers were handed in to her although, I have to admit, not regularly. Vera printed encouraging personal messages on their work, stuck bright stickers here and there, and always returned the envelopes by the following week. She often included little Bible story picture cards that were eagerly taped onto bedroom doors. Her interest kept my boys interested. They finished the three years of primary lessons in good order.

"All the parents got their children started on the home religion program," Vera told me, "but your three were the only ones who finished it."

When the boys were older, Vera signed up to be Prayer Sponsor for all three of them while they were preparing for First Communion. She had been praying for us ever since, and our family needed her prayers now, more than ever before. It was very important to me that she be involved in Alex's funeral.

She promised to help spread the pall.

Maddy and her husband were ex foster parents. Their home had been open during the same years we had fostered.

She remembered the annual picnics and Christmas parties put on by the local Foster Parents Association, with hordes of little children running loose, and Alex among them thoroughly enjoying himself. She even remembered his cuteness the year our family presented a St. Nicholaas play.

Kathleen had been the Narrator of our little drama. James had enjoyed being Black Pete, going down the chimney with presents from St. Nicholaas to put into the children's shoes. Zanny, Timmy, and Alex were sleeping children. Peter taught us the Dutch words for two St. Nicholaas songs and designed an enormous portable cardboard chimney and fireplace. We practiced often—the little kids were more than willing to rehearse because Black Pete used real candies for props.

Alex, who had recently turned four and was small for his age, knew his part perfectly. He happily went to bed between Zanny and Timmy, facing our practice audience of dolls and teddy bears. He pulled the blanket up under his chin, closed his eyes and proved that he was asleep by snoring loudly, while Black Pete filled his shoe and went back up the chimney. He awoke on cue and ran to see what St. Nicholaas had sent. He remembered to sit on the floor and take the candies out of his shoe one at a time. He had memorized all the words for "Zie Ginds Komt de Stoomboot" and "Dank U Sinterklaasje" although the tunes escaped him.

Two days before the Foster Families Christmas party we held a very successful dress rehearsal at school for Timmy's and Zanny's kindergarten class. And when the big afternoon finally arrived, Alex captivated his audience, first by sleeping and snoring with his large sparkling eyes wide open and then by tipping his shoe up over his head and shaking it to be sure the last candy was out.

Allen was a fellow church member and longtime family friend who had been a teacher at Lomas Elementary School. He remembered another Christmas and a project he had given his grade three class the year he taught Alex. The children had been told to write "A Christmas Story." Every child, with the exception of ours, had written about Santa and his reindeer, stockings, Christmas trees, and presents. Alex had written about Mary and Joseph, baby Jesus, the shepherds, and the three wise men.

"Alex was very shy—never volunteering information and reluctant to answer questions," said Allen. "As a result, I tended not to put him under any pressure during class discussions. But he was a nice child, happy and quiet, and his manners were impeccable."

Alex's Godparents, Patricia and Graham, had a much more recent incident to share. They made specialty candles and sold them at the local markets. Alex, who was one of their regular customers, had candles created by Patricia in every room of his apartment, even the bathroom, each one standing in its own little glass container.

Patricia said, "The last time Alex bought a candle he paid me with change and somehow his ring fell off. I found it in my cash box when we got home and recognized it right away. I put it in an envelope for him."

I asked, hopefully, "Is it the big silver clunker he always wore on a chain around his neck?"

"No, this is the ring he wore on his little finger," explained Patricia.

So, the big ring was still missing. But Tim, for whom those rings had become a major concern, would be glad to know Alex's little ring had turned up.

"I think you should keep it," I said, and over Patricia's protests added, "You guys are his Godparents. It'll be nice for us, knowing you have something to remember him by."

My very elderly friend, Henry, sighed, "I'm really sorry there won't be any more funny stories about Alex. My favourite was his vote at the last election." I knew Henry would bring that up—he always did.

It was the year our federal and provincial elections were held back to back. To add to the confusion, the ridings had been changed. South Prevost Valley and North Prevost Valley were now separated, in typical Canadian fashion, and the usual slate of provincial candidates for the Prevost Valley had therefore doubled. Our local papers gave everybody equal coverage, printing, over three weeks, the pictures, parties, and platforms of all those running for MP or MLA. For Alex's current girlfriend, Louisa, the whole affair had become too complicated.

Louisa was old enough to vote for the first time. She phoned me a few days before the election.

"I don't know who to vote for!" she wailed. "My father said NDP and my mother said Liberal. I want to decide for myself, but there's so many, and I don't understand."

"Why don't you and Alex come for lunch," I said, "and I'll help you sort things out."

After lunch, while Alex read a Tintin, Louisa and I poured over the papers and talked politics. Louisa knew what she wanted; her problem was having to cope with two elections at once. At the end of an hour she was organized, and a pair of small cards were safely in her pocket, each bearing a date, a voting place, and the last name of her favourite candidate.

"What about you, Alex?" I asked as he and Louisa prepared to leave. "Do you know who you are going to vote for?"

"Don't worry about me, Mom," said Alex proudly. "*I'm* voting for George Bush!"

Elliot, who headed up the Social Justice Committee at St. Cecelia's said he would be pleased to do one of the readings at Alex's funeral.

"I'm glad you called me," he said, "because I was about to call you. Have you got time to listen?"

"Yes."

"Good. I wanted to tell you about the dream I had last night. It was so vivid!"

Elliot said he had been shocked when he heard the news of Alex's death, firstly by the unexpected and secondly by the unexplained. He went to bed last night thinking that there had to be a reason for this.

The dream started, he told me, with a totally dark background but swirling mists soon began to cover everything. Suddenly Alex was there, walking out of the mist toward Elliot, smiling, with a lighted candle in his right hand. He said, "It's okay. Don't worry about me. I'm fine."

Elliot was sure this message was not meant only for him because, until now, his dreams had been noticeably silent, and often the next morning, it was hard to remember exactly what had happened.

"But this time the memory stayed with me," he said. "The candle was an important symbol of life and hope but the crucial facts, for me, were that the vision was so clear, the message was so reassuring, and the peace I felt afterwards was so intense."

Veronica, president of the FASD Action Team Society, wasn't home when I called. Later she sent an email.

"I received a phone call from Alex a few weeks ago, asking me to meet him at the Donut Shop. He'd had a fight with his girlfriend and was feeling pretty upset about it. We talked for a while but that was it. A pretty normal reaction, I thought at the time. Shortly after that, I saw him directing people to parking spots at an FASD event. We spoke briefly, but he was busy doing his job. Of course, I will always ask myself if there were cues that I missed…"

"I remember the day I met Alex," said Rachael, St. Cecelia's soloist. "It was soon after we moved to Alderlea when he was working at Liberty's. I knew he was your son, Ruth, so I introduced myself."

Rachael noticed Alex several times while she did her shopping. He was helping the other customers, busily folding untidy clothes, talking to people, and being generally useful. When she got to the cashier, Alex bagged the things she bought and thanked her for shopping there.

"He was a cheerful presence in the store, looking out for others and connecting in that smiling, easy manner he had," Rachael told me. "It will be an honour to sing at his funeral."

Peter came into my office with two cups of coffee. "All these memories," he said sadly. "I've been remembering Alex the day we got him. He was such a tiny little guy, and he was already so good at playing the adults off against each other. I told him to eat his veggies, do you remember? And he held out his arms to you, with that 'poor little me' look. It was hard to be firm."

"Tiny but tough," I said. "Zan and Tim were a year older, but Alex held his own. He was the first to be toilet trained."

Peter managed a small grin. "You would remember their diapers! I remember how scared Alex was of sirens. Police or fire or ambulance, he tried to hide from all of them. We got him that big ride-on fire engine for his second birthday—that helped."

"Zan rode the green alligator, and Timmy rode his horse, and Alex rode on that fire engine," I recalled. "They always travelled single file, being a train. They left dents and gouges in all the cupboard doors."

Those three little fellows had wonderful imaginations. A new hat in the dress up trunk or a handful of plastic straws unexpectedly appearing in their box of dishes under the sink kept them busy for a whole morning. They played together all day, every day, without stress or argument. Zanny was the undisputed leader; Timmy and Alex were contented followers.

"Alex was scared of water, too," Peter reminisced. "Remember how he used to scream bloody murder in the bathtub...especially when you had to wash his hair."

"Oh, and do you remember that time when he slid on a wet rock and fell into the river? He wasn't hurt, but he didn't get up." I shook my head. "The water was only half an inch deep, but he just lay there with his face in it. That was so scary. I tried to run to him, but my legs wouldn't go forward. It took me ages to reach him."

"It took you about two seconds," said Peter. "I couldn't believe how fast you moved!"

Late in the afternoon, I called Clare, my closest friend. Clare and I had first encountered each other twenty-six years ago when I was nursing little Zanny and Clare's youngest was still a toddler. Among many common interests, we had quickly discovered the most important—a shared sense of humour. The prayer group we had started, as a result of our original meeting, was still coming together weekly even though neither Clare nor I could remain involved once school activities began to fill our lives.

As our older children reached the right ages for summer camp, we both became strong supporters of Camp Columbia. I was on the committee for seven years; Clare served for ten. Whenever Clare and I went to a children's weekly camp as staff, we brought our little ones along as Staff Kids. As soon as they were old enough they went to the junior camps, moved on through the intermediate and senior stages, and most of them came back as counsellors or kitchen help or lifeguards in their late teens.

Clare liked being in charge; she always signed up to be a camp Chief. I liked being directed; I preferred the position of assistant Chief, Crafty, or Granny. Going to a camp together was tremendous fun for both of us and we had managed to do that most summers.

These days, we often met at the office of our shared physiotherapist, enduring unpleasant morning appointments and enjoying lunch together, afterwards.

Clare said, "Oh, hello, Lovey. How are you?"

"Reasonable," I answered." Needing to hear your voice, is all."

"I've been thinking about you and Alex all day," said Clare, "and for some reason I keep remembering that special porridge you made for Alex when he was in kindergarten…."

Alex had started kindergarten with all the necessary social skills. Being the youngest of five children, he knew how to charm, how to operate in a crowd, how to get out of doing chores, and how to organize his full share of whatever was going on.

Because he was a bit behind, both mentally and physically, Peter and I made sure he could do up all his buttons and zippers, recognize his own lunchbox, line up, take turns, and choose a partner. We thought he was off to a good start but in mid-September, he brought home a note from his teacher: "Alex isn't able to keep up with the others in circle time because he doesn't know his colours. Can you help him at home?"

I was astounded. How could Alex not know colours? He had

certainly been exposed to them often enough. Eight years ago we had worried about Kathleen, who learned only green and yellow before kindergarten, but within a week of starting school she knew all the colours and began passing on her knowledge to little James. Timmy and Zanny were never taught—they picked up colours and counting and everything else by osmosis. I had assumed it was the same for Alex.

That fall, as well as having five children in elementary school, we had a three month old foster baby waiting for adoption. Kathleen, now in grade seven, needed hours of my help with her schoolwork. Even the grade four homework James had to do required some adult supervision. Pickling and canning and freezing and jam making were in full swing. There would be very little time left over for Alex's colours.

I phoned the kindergarten teacher; together we worked out a strategy.

The following Monday morning was the beginning of Red Week. Alex wore a red shirt borrowed from Zan, he had a red apple in his lunch box, and he carried red flowers for his teacher. The kindergarten class concentrated on red things all week and on Friday at snack time Alex had a treat for all—iced cookies covered with red sugar sprinkles. It was worth my being up half the night to get them ready. 'Red' had been well established.

In succeeding weeks, Alex learned orange, purple, yellow, white, and brown. We skipped pink. Our only pink clothes belonged to Kathleen; she refused to share and Alex was very thankful. He couldn't put a name to 'pink,' but he knew it was a girl's colour. The teacher found Black Week a bit tricky (kindergarten is geared to brighter colours) but Alex loved it. He got to wear James's black Batman shirt all week and he had black licorice every day for snack time. Blue Week turned out to be more difficult; we were stuck in the various shades of blue for several weeks.

On the first Monday morning in December Alex pulled on his dark green sweater, watched Mommy put a green apple and some green celery into his lunch box, and carried a green Christmas cracker to school for Show and Tell. The cracker was a mistake.

Christmas was already in the air and neither Alex nor the other children had any more interest in colours. Green Week dragged. Even Thursday's cookies, shaped like leaves and covered with green icing and green sugar sparkles failed to spark interest. On Thursday night, Alex still didn't know green.

By that time our baby had been adopted and all the preserving was finished but Christmas was coming and Mom, like the kindergarten class, had reached the end. I couldn't face another week of green. It was time for drastic measures.

At our house, each child had some bottled fruit for breakfast, followed by a bowl of oatmeal porridge covered with a little bit of brown sugar and a big scoop of homemade peanut butter granola. On that most memorable morning in our family's history, there was no granola. Instead the oatmeal was bright green. Mom had stirred in some drops of food colouring when no one was looking.

Even now, many years later, the kids still talk about the morning they had to eat green oatmeal, and Tim always adds, "Without granola!" Kathleen has disliked porridge ever since.

But that morning Alex learned the colour green.[1]

---

[1] First published in part as *When Crayons Aren't Enough*. Family Groundwork. (November 2003)

Finding Positives in the Negatives

Anita was chairperson of the Compassion Committee, a group of hard-working volunteers, mostly women, who catered for the funeral receptions of St. Cecelia's parishioners. She called before supper.

"I'm a bit confused," she said. "I've been asked to organize the 'Spencer' funeral, but who has died? As far as I know, the only Spencers at St. Cecelia's are your family."

"Yes," I said. "It's Alex."

"What?" gasped Anita. "Not little Alex?"

Anita was much more than a friend from church. A kindergarten teacher, she had transferred to Lomas School for a year or two before her retirement, and Alex, who was in kindergarten for the second time, had blossomed forth with unexpected strengths and skills under her guidance…

Kathleen and Alex had late fall birthdays; both had started school when they were only four. Neither was mature enough to handle grade one the following September and we had asked for a repeat of kindergarten for Kathleen. Eight years later we made the same request for Alex.

Kathleen's teacher had welcomed our decision. She told me the choice to repeat kindergarten had to come from the parents, not the school, and she had been hoping we would hold Kathleen back. She thought another 'prep' year would give Kathleen a head start in grade one.

But Alex's teacher, while agreeing with us regarding his immaturity, was doubtful about another year of kindergarten. She said Alex already needed extra help, and he wouldn't get that in kindergarten so he should go on. If he needed to repeat a year, let it be grade one. Peter and I completely disagreed, having seen Kathleen's success. Because the school wouldn't cooperate with our choice for Alex, we brought in the big guns—Charles, Alex's social worker. And a decision was made: Alex would be tested. If the results showed immaturity only, Alex would stay in kindergarten. If the results showed an unusual need for remedial help, Alex would start grade one. The results showed both. The determination was left in the hands of Alex's parents. He stayed in kindergarten.

The following September Alex had a different teacher—our friend, Anita. Within a month, we could see changes; Alex switched from his 'little and cute' mindset to 'boy with a mission.' Anita had made him the first class monitor. Not because he had been in kindergarten before, and not because he was the oldest, but because he had 'the very first birthday of the year.'

Alex and Anita had been special friends ever since. In fact, Anita was one of the first people from whom Alex had begged money when he was living on the streets.

Having completely lost her usual composure, Anita started to cry.

"I'm sorry to have dumped it on you like that," I apologized. "I thought everybody already knew."

When Anita had recovered enough to discuss the funeral reception, we hit another snag—she needed numbers, and I could only offer wild guesses.

"For a young person, the church is usually full," said Anita.

"Yes, but many of Alex's friends are almost as dysfunctional as he is and even with having every intention of coming, they might not get there," I explained. "The FASD Society will come, and family, and our friends, and some parishioners. That's maybe half a church. And there's something else that will limit the attendance—the obit won't be out in the local papers till Wednesday, and people who might have come won't know until it's too late. We hope to have the funeral on Tuesday."

"Father Joe has definitely booked it for Tuesday," said Anita.

"Yes, I know, but Joe hasn't got the final say in this case. We might be having some legal intervention."

"Ruth. Tell me the whole story," Anita ordered. When I had finished, she asked, "If we are able to have a funeral, would The Family join in? Would they come to the reception?"

"I don't know."

"Oh well, it's only Friday. We don't have to start organizing anything yet. When will you know more?"

"The coroner said she would phone tonight. I'll call you as soon as I hear anything," I promised, and wrote Anita's name on the lengthening list beside the telephone.

Sherry called after supper. Nothing had changed.

During the evening friends phoned offering help, sympathy, food for the funeral reception, and flowers for the church. Only when it came to the latter did I know exactly what to say. One of Alex's special pleasures had been picking brilliant bouquets of flowers in our garden—tiny daisies with mismatched orange dahlias, or pale pink columbine with bright orange calendula—and taking them to his girlfriends. Alex loved orange.

"Flowers would be wonderful—the brighter the better—but don't go out and buy them," I told all who asked. "Something from your garden would be perfect. And if you could bring them in one of your own vases? And take them home again after the service? The church janitor will bless you forever if she doesn't have to clean up flower mess!"

I was the church janitor.

Back in 1988, when the woman who cleaned the church basement retired, we had accepted the St. Cecelia's Hall janitorial contract. We were always ready to take on family jobs and already held a few neighbourhood paper routes. We also kept up the gardens for several institutions. Once we even picked rocks. Our children had to earn their own spending money; there was nothing extra for allowances in our tight budget. As they got older, obtained summer jobs, and gave up their paper routes, all the extra gardening gradually became their parents' responsibility. Then in 1995, when we were asked to add cleaning the upstairs of the church complex to the contract we already held for the downstairs, I accepted for myself (with Peter's help for the heavy work) and we stopped gardening all over town.

It was getting late when I finally had time to answer Sara's email from the day before. Sara and I had never met face to face. I knew her through her work at the Special Needs Adoptive Parents office in Vancouver. As editor of the quarterly news-magazine published by SNAP[2], she had occasionally asked me to write an article on some aspect of FASD parenting. We became well acquainted through long telephone conversations, during which Sara suggested corrections, and I made the necessary revisions. Now she was editing a book series on special needs adoption, and I had recently completed a new article for one of the books, 'Adoption Piece by Piece: A Toolkit for Parents.' My offering, ironically, was entitled 'Finding Positives in the Negatives.'

Now I needed to ask Sara if 'Finding Positives' was an appropriate contribution to her book in light of Alex's death, an event that was anything but positive.

This article, written a good eight years after counselling for my stress disorder had started, contained enough emotional content to satisfy both Sara and Mary Grace...

Finding Positives in the Negatives

We seemed such an ordinary family. But 'ordinary' was really an illusion. We kept it in place through busyness and denial.

---

[2] First published in "Adoption Piece by Piece: a Toolkit for Parents"

How long did we teeter at the edge of the precipice before we slipped, apparently so suddenly, into the legal system and Corrections? Into mental health services and income assistance? Some of us slid even further, falling right through the social safety net and adjusting easily to carpet surfing, sexual promiscuity, drug and alcohol abuses, and life on the streets.

After that first rapid descent, I supported my adult children with FASD through many disasters—evictions, homelessness, suicide attempts, welfare fraud, arrests and incarcerations, punishments dealt out by local drug dealers, sexually transmitted diseases, trips to Emergency—but I did so without any hope. My bit of the future seemed truly hopeless. One more black-edged precipice. For a long, long time, I defined myself and my family through our losses because our gains, like our disabilities, were invisible.

Now it's sometimes possible for me to step well back from the edge, and to see my kids without those despairing FASD glasses. Sometimes tiny glitterings of hope—small positives—shine through the vast blackness of negatives.

For many years, I supported the local food bank without a thought beyond helping the less fortunate and feeling good about doing it. But now the 'less fortunate' have faces and feelings and friendship to offer, and I need them more than they have ever needed me. My sons eat at the food bank; sometimes they serve their community service hours there. The other regulars are their support group.

Tim, several hours out of jail and due to meet his probation officer in twenty minutes, asked me to make a quick stop at the food bank. It seemed an odd request. Why would he want to go into such a depressing place? He had just finished coffee, fries, and three burgers at a cheerful, upbeat MacDonald's. Lunch at the food bank was only soup and a bun. But Tim said he wasn't interested in more food. He ran up the stairs. Knowing the speed with which this young man can disappear, I hurried along behind him and was in time to catch the stunned silence of the diners, followed by their roar of welcome. Cups and spoons were banged on the tables. Small children left their places and ran across the room for hugs. A fast round of handshakes, Tim's arm encircling the thin shoulders of two sulky teenage boys, a quick "see you tomorrow," and we were on our way.

Tim was more relaxed than he had been all morning. I felt humbled. Had his own family, much as we loved him, ever given him this kind of a welcome home? At the same time, it was comforting to know that my son was valued and appreciated by others. However disastrous their circumstances, however poorly managed their lives, however dysfunctional their families, these people were Tim's community, and they were delighted to have him back.

Alex, my very self absorbed youngest, has learned to manage his life in other ways. He is fascinated by illnesses, particularly his own. His concentration on his own body is complete. Alex takes every rash, every bruise, every sliver, every pimple, every pain straight to Emergency. He even called an ambulance for himself one day after he stubbed his toe.

Killing time in the Emergency waiting room is a pleasure for my son. He meets his friends there, other adults with FASD who are as self-absorbed as he is and as much in need of mothering. Weekends are favourite times for developing a headache, stomachache or backache because the Friday and Saturday night traffic accidents bring spiraling excitement into Emergency, and it's always fun to be the first to know.

But Alex and his friends are also the first to offer coffee and sympathy. They collect in crowds to be with their friends in times of crisis—even 'friends' they hardly know. Their emotions flow over each other freely, laughter and tears in equal proportions. Right now, in this present moment, they really, really care. I was unusually proud of Alex last winter. For two weeks he walked to the hospital every day to talk to an old man, "About your age, Mom," who had no other visitors.

I focused on my daughter's difficult partner—learning disabled, bipolar, drug addicted—and finally began to appreciate that my daughter has been off welfare and self-supporting for five whole years. Not only that, her relationship and sobriety have lasted for eight years. For those of us who understand, hers is an amazing FASD success story.

And there are other sorts of successes.

In the mental health and addiction subculture, anybody with a roof offers floor space to friends and acquaintances. Tim has often taken advantage of this generosity. When he happens to have an apartment himself, he never locks his door because "Somebody might need my bed."

Recently Tim discovered a little twelve year old, a group home escapee, asleep on his couch. This child lived with Tim, unsupervised, until the group home staff caught up with him. I expressed horror, but Tim said, "It wasn't my job to look after him. And he had to live somewhere." Right on both counts. My son has an enviable ability to provide for his friends' needs while minding his own business.

When Tim is being 'corrected,' my focus is on the painfulness of incarceration; I haven't looked for achievements in jail. But the guards notice. They have told me about my son's politeness, his friendliness, his lack of self-pity, his support for the underdog, his leadership skills, and, especially, his ability to coordinate recreational floor-hockey games in such a way that no playing time is wasted and everybody has fun.

And Alex, although obsessing about his own health, gives family members equal time. He anxiously phones all his siblings if Mom or Dad is ill; he even brings us get well cards, always signed "from your son Alex Spencer." I appreciate Alex's keeping me inside the loop; he is the one who calls Mom whenever Tim's lifestyle sends him back to either hospital or jail.

But the most surprising, and certainly the most exceptional positive in the lives of my brain-damaged children is their inability to hold grudges. This is combined with an equally wonderful desire to forgive and forget.

Tim's best friend, Red, pushed him down a flight of stairs during a spat over a girl, causing a compound fracture of Tim's ankle. My son will always have a slight limp. He can participate, carefully, in soccer and floor hockey, but there is no point in trying to run when the police arrive. However, he and Red are still best friends.

Alex, my paranoid son, decided he was "being stalked" by Randy, an FASD acquaintance. He put in a charge and the whole thing actually went through the courts. The judge added a few months to Randy's already extensive probation order and gave him some community work hours. Six weeks later Alex and Randy found themselves living in the same apartment building, and now Randy is over at Alex's place daily, using the phone.

I think this special capacity to forgive is my children's most powerful lifestyle choice; it's a light shining through all the darkness in their lives.

Clothes for the Burning

Emptying out a home after a death is an unpleasant task. Peter and I had already done it twice in the last six months and we were not looking forward to another round. In rented places, it was necessary to work quickly, and to be decisive to the point of ruthlessness. Empty boxes were always hard to get hold of, organizing storage was always tricky, and emotions had to be shelved for the duration.

Willie, our sister-in-law, had lived here in Alderlea. When she died, Lucy and Fons took on all the paperwork because their home was over on the mainland, and Peter and I did the physical labour because we lived close by. Willie's place was crammed with possessions, and, unfortunately, rented. That was my first experience of having to empty a house in a hurry. All the photographs and documents and sentimental memorabilia went to Lucy. Clothes were packed and dropped off at the Goodwill. Many, many boxes of food, tools, linens, electrical equipment, and general household items from Aunty Willie's place were handed on to James, Zan, Tim, and Alex. Kathleen missed out, being up in Kimberly. Fons and Lucy's kids didn't want anything.

Then our friend Mildred died. She lived in a small unit at The Rainbow, one of the Lutheran establishments for the elderly in Victoria. She died late on a Saturday night and her rooms had to be ready for a new occupant by Monday morning. For Peter and me, her executors, it was another rush job. We left a pile of clothing on the bed for the Lutheran Thrift Shoppe downstairs, stored some personal items, photos, and jewellery for her nephew, and once more packed up dishes and linens, books and records, small furnishings and pictures for our four boys.

Now we would have to do it all again for Alex. And all the things that Alex had inherited from Willie and Mildred would have to be organized and packed for a second time.

"Remind me to go home the long way," I directed Tim as we drove to Alex's apartment on Saturday morning. "I forgot and came into town past the Big House again. They've started another meeting and there are even more cars now than yesterday. I start to feel sick with nerves passing that place."

"I feel sick thinking about going to Alex's apartment without Alex," Tim complained. "What do we have to get?"

"Old clothes for burning—one of everything, same as yesterday—and shoes."

"I saw his good runners in the bedroom, but we should keep those. They might fit Zan or me."

"Good plan. No point in burning clothes that can be used. And I guess all Alex's things belong to us, now."

This was clearly a new idea for Tim. He mulled it over while I parked the car.

"Mom? Do you think I could have Alex's toaster oven?"

"Yes, of course. Look around while we're there and see what else you can use," I advised, glad to shift the conversation to a slightly more positive topic.

But it was hard to go into Alex's apartment, and even harder to sort through his drawers, looking for worn out T-shirts and underwear. Yesterday, the things we needed had been on the surface. Today I had to dig. Being a mother, I stopped to refold clothing and to match and roll socks, finishing with one pair without heels and three singles.

"Might as well send all of these. They're no use to anyone," I said, passing the socks and two ripped T-shirts to Tim, who was holding the bag and waiting for Mom to do the work. "We have to get some pants. Let's check out the closet."

The day before, Tim had retrieved the necessary clothing, but now he backed off, and I got my first look inside Alex's closet. Twice the size of the one Peter and I shared, it was solidly packed with hangers and every hanger was in service.

"It's not all his," Tim offered indifferently.

"Who else owns it?"

"I don't know. He borrows and trades with his friends. I think those are Frankie's shirts," pointing to three with long sleeves in the middle of the bar. "And these are mine," he added, indicating several colourful hockey jerseys at the far end of the closet.

"Why are they here?"

"I gave them to Alex; they were all too small for me. But I'm going to take them home now, before those Indians get them," and Tim unhooked the jerseys and carefully placed all six on the bed.

"You can quit worrying; The Family won't be coming here," I said, but Tim remained unconvinced.

"Somebody was here. Those wolves are gone."

"Anyway, there's a bit more space now. Let's take Frankie's shirts out, too," I suggested. "We can drop them off at his place on our way past. And here are some jeans with ripped knees, but how do we know if they're Alex's? They might belong to somebody else."

"Who cares?" growled Tim. "They're in Alex's closet: they're his." I dropped the jeans into the bag and looked around for shoes.

"Are you going to try on those runners?"

"Next time." Tim could hardly wait to get out of there.

"Okay, they'll have to do without shoes; we'll take Alex's rickety old sandals, instead. Do you want to bring the toaster oven now?"

"No," said Tim. He was already heading for the door with the bag of clothes for burning in one hand, hockey jerseys in the other, and tears streaming down his face.

We were barely home when the phone began to ring. "Hello, Ruth." It was Sherry, taking a quick break from the fourth family meeting. "How are you?"

"All right. Tim and I just got back from Alex's place. We collected some of his clothes for the Burning and dropped them off at the funeral home."

"That must have been hard for both of you." She waited, but I had nothing to add. "Where is Tim now?"

"He's here because Suzanne had to work today. He and Peter are starting some digging in the garden. How are things at your end?"

"I'm using every arbitration skill I ever learned at law school," sighed Sherry, "and so far nothing much has changed. Ruth, I know Alex didn't have a will, but you said he did a lot of writing. I'm wondering if he ever wrote anything about his own funeral?"

"Not that I know of."

"Too bad," said Sherry regretfully. "One sentence in his own handwriting saying he wanted his mom and dad to be in charge of his funeral and this whole problem would be solved."

"That's all we would have needed?"

"Yes."

"I'll tell Kathleen and Tim," I promised. "They'll both be glad to know there is something they can do to prevent anything like this happening to them. Tim will probably write his today."

Such a simple little step. If only we had known.

The next call was from Zan. "Hi, Mom. I have some bad news."

"Don't tell me you can't come this afternoon!"

"Relax, I'm coming," said Zan. "I'm phoning to let you know Conner can't be a pall bearer for Alex."

"That's too bad. Why not?"

"His father died the day after Alex. He had a heart attack."

"Oh Zan, I'm so sorry." Conner and Zan had been best friends ever since they had started grade eight together. During the time his own family was in turmoil, Zan, with my encouragement, had practically lived over at Conner's place. He had camped with Conner and his brothers, learned how to play golf with them, and had been taught how to hunt by their father. Conner's family was as familiar to Zan as his own, and he was very fond of Conner's dad.

"How's Conner doing?"

"We only talked on the phone. I haven't seen him," said Zan. "He sounded all right. I'm going to stop at his mom's place this afternoon."

"Are you okay?" I asked and could have kicked myself. He had lost both his youngest brother and a special friend. Of course he wasn't okay.

Planning the Funeral

Zan had returned from New Zealand three weeks earlier, delighted with his working year abroad and filled with new plans and ambitions. Typical of Zan, he had left his mountain bike behind with a penniless friend and had arrived carrying an enormous extra suitcase full of expensive, well thought out gifts for each member of the family. He also brought with him a full year's growth of reddish blond hair, parted in the centre, flowing in waves down below his collar, and styled by the wind. His beard, however, had been kept neatly trimmed. Our friends told us he looked "just like Jesus."

When we met him in St. Cecelia's parking lot that afternoon, I was relieved to note a new haircut but sorry to see his strained expression. Zan was only twenty-six; today he looked much older. Being a man who believed that speech was silver but silence was golden, he gave Mom and Dad a brief greeting, an even briefer hug, and led the way toward the church.

Father Joe was waiting for us in his office. He hugged me, gripped Peter's shoulder, and shook hands with Zan, welcoming him back to Canada.

He had been in touch with Stanley at Generations—"Twice," he told us—and was aware of the stand being taken by The Family. He wanted to know our position. Peter was clearly aggrieved. Zan shrugged.

"I'm feeling caught in the middle," I said.

As far as the politics were concerned—all the fourth, fifth, and sixth cousins who never knew Alex but were now demanding their 'rights'—I agreed with Peter. That part was decidedly difficult. But some of The Family members were Alex's closest relatives; they had bonded with him when he was a tiny baby and had always cared about him. These were the same people who had suffered the death of Alex's birth father a couple of years before. Several of them were my friends.

"We know some of Alex's aunts and uncles. I wish we could be planning *with* them, or at least talking," I lamented, "instead of having all this friction."

"I never knew Alex very well," said Joe. "But didn't he serve at the altar last Christmas?"

Peter and I smiled at each other, pleased that Alex was remembered. He had phoned us at the last moment on Christmas morning…could we stop by and pick him up on our way to church? We did, and we had barely settled ourselves in the last row on the left side—our favourite spot—when one of the ushers who had known Alex all his life asked him if he would take the place of a missing altar boy. Alex was thrilled. Right up there in front of God and everybody, and on Christmas morning, too. Even though it had been about seven years since he had last been an altar server, he remembered all the tasks and did them with flair.

"Tell me more about him," invited Father Joe.

Two copies of Alex's obituary were in my folder; I handed one to Joe and the other to Zan but retreated from the discussion that followed. I had to admire Joe's wisdom, though. Talking about Alex brought Peter past his irritation with Alex's birth family and gave Zan an opening to share some 'big brother' stories.

When all three of us were a little more relaxed, Joe opened the top drawer of his desk and took out one of his standard funeral forms. He flipped through to the Personal Information section.

"Your turn, Ruth," he said, his bright blue eyes twinkling at me across the table.

"Mothers are good at remembering all the names and numbers."

Zan looked astonished when I rattled off Alex's baptism and

confirmation dates and Peter looked equally astonished when he heard Kaitlyn's birth date. "I thought she was still a baby," he muttered to himself. But I was stumped when we came to Alex's present address. Zan and Peter didn't know it, either.

"It's his third place this year. I know where it is," I said.

"I could drive you right to it," added Peter, "but I don't know the name of the street or the building."

"Don't worry, I'll write 'apartment,'" said Joe, "and I'll put your home address under Family Contact." He turned back to the page marked Preservice Planning, with its first section already written up, and looked at us over the top of his glasses.

"We're going to plan this service as you would have wanted it if there hadn't been any interference," he said, "because you people need to have things settled. If there are a few changes later, well, we can deal with that."

He had checked off Funeral Mass, which assumed that Alex would be present, rather than Memorial Service, which assumed that he wouldn't. The spaces for date, time, place, and presider were already filled in.

"You'll need six pallbearers."

"We're working on it," said Zan. "You can write down me and Tim and Uncle Bruce and Frankie August."

Father Joe did so. "We usually reserve the first three rows of chairs for the pallbearers and the family," he said. "Will that be enough?"

"Who knows?" said Peter. "It depends on how many people think they are family. But that's room enough for us."

Father Joe tapped the next section with his pen. "Do you want the choir?"

"No thanks," I said. "Most of the people who are in the choir now never knew Alex. We've talked to Rachael and Linda; if we're allowed to have a funeral, they'll do the music for us." I passed an index card across the table. "They already know which hymns we want. Here's the list."

Two of our choices weren't in *Breaking Bread*, the parish hymnal, but I planned to print off about seventy five copies of each and would ask someone to hand them out at the door, along with the hymn books.

"Ruth chose the hymns, and I chose two readings," said Peter. "We did that the first morning."

Father Joe looked unconvinced. Hymns were all very well, but he wasn't about to include anything else in his liturgies unless it had received his personal stamp of approval. He and Peter got busy with their Bibles. Eventually, both of Peter's scripture choices were accepted and the names of the two friends we had previously asked to do the readings were added to the funeral plan. Father Joe, himself, would choose the Gospel.

Three people who had been mandated for St. Cecelia's, and who were coming to the funeral in any case, had already agreed to serve as Ministers of the Eucharist. I gave Joe their names and then pointed out another complication.

Most of Alex's friends were unchurched. They would follow the leader. When the people in front of them went forward for communion they would go too, without any understanding of what it was all about. Many of them would be experiencing their First Communion at Alex's funeral.

"If these kids are offered a cup of wine, they won't understand to take a little sip and hand the cup back," I warned. "The first one to get there will probably glug down the whole thing. I think for this occasion it would be best to have only the bread."

"I agree with you," said Joe emphatically.

Our family had already decided against having a traditional prayer vigil for Alex the night before the funeral. For one thing, that would be the Monday evening of the May long weekend, a busy time for most people, especially those who were getting their vegetable gardens planted. For another, encounters with The Family were draining our energy. We didn't have the emotional strength to organize anything extra.

Father Joe had problems of his own. Most of his parishioners had the bodies of their loved ones brought to the church the evening before the funeral; Catholics held their vigils or 'wakes' in their churches, not at funeral homes. Afterwards, bodies were left inside the church overnight. But after talking with Stanley, Joe had serious doubts regarding the security of the church complex.

"The way things are going right now," said Zan, "we probably wouldn't be allowed to have a prayer vigil even if we wanted one."

Father Joe checked through his list for anything he might have missed. "Had you planned to have a eulogy?" he asked.

"No," said Peter. Some priests were open to having a eulogy at the beginning of a funeral before the service actually started, but we knew Father Joe was not one of these. He expected eulogies to happen either at the prayer vigil the night before or at the reception following the funeral. Peter and I disliked the whole concept of the reception eulogy. By that time, people were holding coffee or tea in one hand and a little plate of sandwiches in the other hand; they were connecting with friends and searching for a place to sit. They were ready to relax. We felt this wasn't the time to insist on more long speeches, especially in St. Cecelia's hall, which housed a dreadful echo.

"Alex wrote his Life Story for the FASD Action Team website and it was also published in the SNAP Newsmagazine," I told Joe, handing him another paper. There was a pile collecting on his side of the desk. "We want to give out copies of that at the reception, instead of having a eulogy."

"Good idea." Father Joe put a line through 'Eulogy' and added, "Have you been in touch with Anita about the food? She'll need numbers."

"I talked to her," I said, "and we can take a guess as far as family and friends are concerned, but we have no idea how many of Alex's birth family would want to come to the church or the reception."

"Or if we'll even be having a reception," said Zan.

"Or a funeral," said Peter.

"Stay positive," said Father Joe.

Flickering Coals

Later that afternoon, while Zan and Peter took the dogs for a long walk, I went to our guest room where Tim had left Alex's two big boxes of papers and started sorting through the jumble.

Soon Alex's cartons were empty, my yellow recycling bags were full, and the bed was dotted with semi organized piles of letters and notes, bills and receipts, magazine pictures and newspaper clippings, old school awards, a library book, and on the pillow a heap of photographs. The photographs were what mattered most. I stacked the rest of Alex's paper into a much smaller box —representing several more hours of work for Mom—and took that and the photos back to my office.

Specially valuable to me were pictures of Kaitlyn. Alex had handfuls of them, mostly doubles and even some triples, all taken during her first year. I separated out the pictures that were of Kaitlyn by herself. Most were familiar, but there were about ten I had never seen before. I slipped those inside the cover of my Brag Book. A good mix of the duplicates was put aside for Kathleen, who hadn't ever met Kaitlyn in person. The rest were sealed in a manila envelope for Alex's birth grandmother.

Photos of Kaitlyn with her uncles, Kaitlyn with her parents, and Kaitlyn with Peter and me were separated with judicial fairness into four equal piles for Kathleen, James, Zan, and Tim.

Alex still had the snapshots of himself as a child and as a young adult that I had given him over the years. It was a surprise to me that he hadn't lost them during one of his many moves. These were first added to the piles going out to the other kids, but then I changed my mind and put them into an envelope marked 'for Kaitlyn.'

Alex's old, corner curled photographs of various cars and cats went directly into my office shredder, and from there to recycling. As I was taking the yellow bags out to the back porch, ready for next week's pick up, the phone rang.

It was Sherry, calling from the Big House.

Yesterday she had shown Alex's immediate birth family his adoption papers and now all the people at Tzouhalem Big House knew he had been officially adopted. In spite of this new information, the political group was still demanding a court injunction. Sherry had explained, more than once, that they hadn't a hope of winning their case, even in Supreme Court, and the rest of The Family were finally starting to accept this.

"I told them about our meeting at Generations and all the concessions you and Peter are willing to make," she said. "Now they are talking about some concessions of their own and the possibility of a burial in Alderlea rather than in Campbell River. It will take a long time—everyone who is here gets to have an opinion, and…"

"Do you want my opinion?" I interrupted. Going through Alex's photographs had been a mistake; my composure had been left somewhere in the recycling.

"I don't care anymore!" I almost shouted. "They can do whatever they want."

"I can certainly understand why you feel that way," Sherry said soothingly, "but let's give the whole situation a bit more time. Some of the elders have already spoken and they have all agreed with your idea of using St. Paul's. I think the rest of The Family are slowly starting to swing against the political faction, but it might take all night. We have to give them time," she repeated.

"Yeah, right," I muttered, then added more politely, "I do appreciate that you are willing to give so much of *your* time to this."

"It's worth it, Ruth. Don't forget we are fighting for Alex's right to have a timely burial."

Sherry certainly knew which buttons to push. I had been advocating for Alex (and fighting for his rights) for the last twenty three years and now I felt my crusader mindset click into place.

"Okay," I said. "We wait. It's a good thing Alex has you on his side."

After Sherry's call I couldn't settle. Her latest report had been disturbing and the photos of little Alex were still hanging in my mind. Peter and Zan weren't back; the house was quiet and very empty.

I picked up the phone and pressed in Mary Grace's home number, knowing she wasn't there, knowing I had nothing to say, but needing to hear her voice, even on the answering machine.

"You have reached Mary Grace, at…"

And suddenly I did have something to say—the words were there, ready to use, without any planning or preparation on my part.

"You know what's the best thing about this whole mess?" I began abruptly. "Alex doesn't have an FASD anymore. He's complete. His brain damage is gone."

I replaced the receiver slowly, adjusting myself carefully to a new feeling of tranquility. Alex had won his battle.

Cricket called before supper. "I was thinking about Alex," she said, "and I remembered something. One night, when me and him couldn't sleep, we talked about our funerals. There was a band Alex really liked—Guns N' Roses. He wanted some of their music played at his funeral."

"I'm glad you thought of it," I said cautiously. "Is it the kind of thing a mother would like?"

"Not very. It has some swears in it. But I know Alex wanted it."

"Do you think he would have anything by this band in his apartment?" I asked.

"He should; he used to play stuff from Guns N' Roses all the time. He had *Use Your Illusion*. That's an album," Cricket added, remembering my ignorance when it came to her kind of music. "Alex especially liked 'November Rain' and 'Don't Cry' and 'Knocking on Heaven's Door.'"

"This is one of those little cassettes that pop into a ghetto blaster, right? I'll look for it tomorrow," I promised. "If it's not there, Tim might have the same thing at his place or maybe we can buy it."

Cricket thought it might be easier to buy a Guns N' Roses album in Calgary than in Alderlea, especially on a long weekend. She would organize a search, she said, and find out about courier services.

I promised to see what could be set up at the church. Father Joe wouldn't mind a taped song being played at the end of the funeral service as long as he had heard it ahead of time. But would he approve something that "had some swears in it?" Never having heard this Guns N' Roses band for myself, nor any of the music my children enjoyed if it could possibly be avoided, I was now at a bit of a loss.

After dinner I went to my office and closed the door, always a sign to the family that Mom needed writing privacy. There were new emails waiting to be read and other emails waiting to be answered, but first my journal needed updating. I was struggling with some FASD issues and writing always helped me clarify my thinking…

The young folks in Alex's FASD mentorship group had reacted to his death in a surprising way. I had expected them to be distressed, but they weren't. In their minds, Alex had acted very selfishly. He had cheated; he had double crossed them; he had let the team down. They were furious.

One of my concerns was the disproportionate number of anxious telephone calls I was receiving from the other FASD parents. We had agonized together and supported one another as special needs adoptive parents for nearly ten years—long before our FASD Society had developed—and we were like a family, having so much adversity and disaster in common.

We had shared the alarm of finding empty beds when our young adolescents first began their nighttime wanderings, the dismay of uncovering teenage drug and alcohol parties, and the betrayal of the petty thefts that went on at home. At our first meeting we discovered one of the things we had in common—our bedroom keys hanging on chains around our necks.

We had all realized, over time, that school suspensions were next to useless. The kids got the suspensions, but the parents got the punishment. Hoping Tim would come to regret his latest debarment from school, I sent him out one April morning to shovel manure over the vegetable garden. His father and I hoped that several hours of heavy work at home would be far more unpleasant for him than deskwork at school. It wasn't. He loved physical labour. The sun was shining, a radio hanging on the fence was blaring, his work was finished in an hour and he came inside to ask what else he could do. My whole day was given over to keeping Tim busy. On the following Monday, I told the principal that any future school suspensions would have to be served at school. The teachers did the suspending—they could also do the necessary monitoring.

Those of us having to deal with the Ministry of Children and Families (often ironically called McFam) were nervous of social workers with high expectations, low acceptance levels, a strong belief in the perfection of their own training, and constant use of "You should…" or "He really must…" Independence at nineteen was their goal for every child, but we already knew our kids with FASD were going to need significant amounts of parental support all their lives. One family had adopted their foster daughter, simply "to keep her safe from those social workers."

Most of us had entered the legal system while our children were still in their teens, Tim and I being the group's pioneers. Our sons' first offences were settled out of court, with automatic community service hours, a compulsory letter of apology sent to the victim, and the acquisition of a probation officer. (At Tim's school, having your own personal probation officer was considered a status symbol.) Unfortunately, kids with FASD don't learn from their mistakes. Their second offences and their first real arrests quickly followed, bringing police cars to our driveways, strangers to our doors, a constant ringing of our phones, curious neighbours, and family uproar.

Together, we learned the mysteries of the legal system and corrections. We all encountered and were outraged by the duty counsels who advised our guys to plead "not guilty," even though all knew they *were* guilty. We joined the ongoing struggle to find lawyers, crown counsels, and judges who were willing to be educated in FASD 101. We discussed a new worry—what to say in court?—supposing we were allowed to say anything. Clothes for court weren't a problem. A speaker at one our FASD meetings had told us what not to wear (skin and leather) and had encouraged us to dress formally. After that, a nice grey suit was passed from mother to mother as we had our days in court.

Some of our sons, now juvenile delinquents, were sent on from youth correctional centres to group homes. In those days, group home staff members were trained in behaviour management and the use of consequences. Being late for the 10 p.m. curfew, with the consequence of being locked out all night, was supposed to teach the boys to get themselves in on time. All it taught our kinds of kids was to be late again the next night because the freedom of the city streets delighted them. Unauthorized trips away from the group home created the consequence of being grounded. Being grounded meant being monitored all the next day. This was supposed to be a punishment, but our boys loved it. Relieved of the burden of responsibility, they basked in hours of undivided staff attention. But even then the staff didn't get it. They continued with behaviour management and blamed the boys' parents, who weren't even there, when it didn't work. We couldn't make them understand that our boys had brain damage and were unable, not unwilling, to learn to manage their own behaviours.

Some of us had to absorb the bleakness of visiting a son in an adult correctional centre—the bare walls, thick bars, bulletproof glass dividers, drab uniforms, unhappy people, and real guns in real holsters. There were many rules for visitors, different in every institution. My first visit to an adult jail happened right after Easter. I had baked my children's favourite sugar cookies—little yellow ducks, white geese with orange feet, and pink and blue rabbits, all covered with candy sprinkles—and had brought them to the prison in Nanaimo. But they weren't allowed; they had to be taken back home, untasted. A year later, visiting at the Burnaby penitentiary, Peter and I were permitted to bring in a big box of birthday gifts, and nobody in authority even looked at them. Security in Canadian correctional centres got tighter after the attack on the World Trade Centre in New York. During a visit to the Wilkinson Road jail in

Victoria, soon after 9/11, Peter and I both got into trouble when Peter forgot to leave his handkerchief with his hat and wallet in the visitors' lockers. In that jail, visitors weren't allowed to reach into their pockets for anything.

Youth probation officers, who positioned themselves to be part of the punishment rather than uniting with the family to be part of the support system, were another problem we had all faced. One P.O. said straight out, "I'm a revolving door sending these kids back to jail." But some of the probation officers assigned to adult offenders were far more understanding. They didn't worry about regular appointments, but opened their offices one or two days each week for a general check in. People on probation who forgot their regular weekly or bi-monthly visits were reminded by phone, rather than being arrested for breach. These probation officers stayed on friendly terms with our sons after their time had been served and were available for things like references and advice. One of the many training workshops put on by our society, 'FASD and the Legal System,' included a panel of three guest speakers: Tim, his mother, and his probation officer.

Our adult kids were evicted regularly, usually because of unpaid rent or all night partying. They weren't bothered; they ate at the food bank and bedded down wherever they happened to be. But as parents, we never became accustomed to their carpet surfing and street living. Whenever one of our lot was homeless we all worried about sleeping arrangements until he (or she) was regrouped, and the mother also worried about clothes and shoes (and jackets in the winter months), but none of us spared a thought for any other belongings. We all knew those would be left behind.

Trips to Emergency were commonplace. For Peter and me, it was mostly broken bones and stitches when our children were little, followed by mental health issues, drug overdose, and crisis surgeries, as they grew older. Other parents dealt with other problems, but we were all used to hospital staff who didn't want to hear about FASD because it wasn't part of the immediate problem. They didn't understand how often FASD could jeopardize a successful medical outcome. They hadn't seen a cast casually removed from a broken hand the day after it had been applied because the owner wanted to go swimming. But one surgeon who had done a tricky internal repair on our son's bowel, perforated by a metal toed boot, actually paid attention. Peter and I said, "He's too sick to move right now, but he's a wanderer with no impulse control. He'll be off down the street the minute he is allowed to get up. You'll have to watch him." Nobody had time to babysit an adult, of course, but the surgeon found a solution. He didn't allow my son's catheter to be removed until an hour before his official discharge.

Some of us were told about the sexually transmitted diseases our sons and daughters had attracted—other parents were blessed with ignorance. Pregnancies were harder to hide. For our daughters, and for our sons' girlfriends, pregnancies were neither calm nor worry free. Emotionally and financially, anything that could possibly go wrong did. We supported wherever we could. Our hopes were basic: we worked for grandchildren born without an FASD.

And now these parents were facing another disaster, the death of one of our own. Until this week, I had thought jail time and unhealthy pregnancies were pretty much the worst that could happen, but now I knew better. And my friends, who also had sons and daughters with an FASD, were terrified of the possibility of copycat suicides.

My incoming computer mail contained some good news for Peter. His sister, Lucy, was doing well after her surgery and her doctor was claiming success. He said all the cancer had been removed.

Cricket, a thoughtful little person, had peppered my inbox and lightened my evening with several silly jokes. I appreciated her effort. It was good to spend a few moments with something cheerful.

There were messages about Alex from an interesting mix of family, friends, total strangers, and institutions: Malaspina College Tutors, the Community Options Society, our FASD government funder from National Crime Prevention, St. John's Anglican Church Women, our local Member of Parliament. Alex had an enormous circle of acquaintances. With no hobbies, few sustainable interests, and sporadic employment, he could put most of his time into building relationships.

Sara, from Special Needs Adoptive Parents, had sent a long, very supportive letter, covering all my email anxiety of the evening before.

> Hi Ruth.
> Good to see your voice in the midst of what must be a crazy, upsetting time. Relieved to know that you're managing to hang in there in spite of everything, somehow. To answer your questions:
> I'd still like to use "Finding Positives." I think it's still very appropriate. It speaks from where you were at when you wrote it, Ruth—there was no way you could have known what was coming around the bend. And that place you were at was just as valid and real as the place you find yourself in now. I think "Finding Positives" will touch and help a lot of other parents—please know that your writing has always been a gift to others who are struggling with similar problems. What happened next does not invalidate what you had to say.
> My question to you is: do you feel OK if I still publish it in the book? If so, do you want me to publish it as is, with no further comment? Or do you want me to add a postscript (which either you or I could write) explaining what's happened since?
> Just continue to write whatever needs to be said.
> Yes, this is undoubtedly an FASD event, and I'm sure you have a lot to process through your writing around this, and yes, it's entirely appropriate. And definitely, yes—people want to know. People need to know. So scream it from the rooftops, do whatever you need to do. This tragedy (as you, yourself, know) was entirely preventable. It goes right back to drinking alcohol during pregnancy, and these stories need to keep being told. I'm just so sorry that Alex's has such a tragic ending.

> You know what, Ruth? I'm relieved to hear that you feel compelled to write about this. From what I know of you, I sense that the writing will help carry you through this very difficult time. So just trust the process. (And feel free to share your writing with me if that helps.)
> Be really gentle with yourself, Ruth. Please know that you are in my heart and my prayers.
> Love, Sara

Once again, a letter from Sara brought me almost to the edge of tears. I wondered how she did it. How could she have access to my emotions when they weren't available to me? It seemed as though both Sara and Mary Grace were reading off the same page, and I didn't even know how to open the book.

My response was short and careful.

> Hi Sara.
> Go ahead and use "Finding Positives," but please don't mention anything about Alex's death. I think that needs to be said at a different time.

I moved the mouse to click 'send' and paused. Neither Sara nor anybody else at SNAP knew what we were going through with Alex's birth family and yet this whole dilemma was clearly an adoption issue. In my opinion, the SNAP office needed to be aware. A warning about the possibility of birth family involvement after the death of an adopted child should go out to other adoptive parents as soon as possible. I continued my letter to Sara in a new vein:

> As well as losing a son and organizing a funeral that will accommodate Alex's street friends with FASD, and suddenly having to learn about 'Suicide and the Legal System,' we have come to a brand new adoption experience. (Well, new for us.) Too bad it's too late to add this to your manual.
> Alex's birth family wants his body, and they

are working on ways to get it. The coroner is having quite a time because part of her job is to make sure appropriate disposal of the body has happened. She has already attended four angry Big House meetings (with hundreds of birth family members present) trying to get things sorted out. She released Alex from the hospital morgue twice already, then had to un-release him because some members of The Family have threatened to steal his body.

My husband and I, who also want the body, had to prove that Alex was adopted. It's a good thing we knew where to find the papers!

This whole event is not going the way our family would have chosen. We have had to make any number of compromises regarding Alex's funeral and burial arrangements because there is still time for a court injunction to go through and that would leave Alex languishing in a fridge for months waiting for a court date. We are legally Alex's parents, and we would win if it came to a trial, but we would rather have Alex properly buried now than win later.

Other adoptive parents need to know about this—it could happen to them.

Ruth

Alex's Last Flame

Tim and I had arranged to meet at Alex's place on Sunday morning at 10. Tim wanted to lay claim to Alex's toaster oven. I wanted both of us to make a start on some of the clearing out and cleaning up. May's rent was paid (Alex had been on 'rent direct' through his disability coverage) giving us two weeks to complete the task. This would have been plenty of time in ordinary circumstances, but these circumstances were far from ordinary. I didn't want to be alone at the apartment, neither did Tim, and Peter wasn't about to do any packing or organizing. "Let the Building Manager do it," was all he had to offer.

When I arrived at Alex's building, Tim was waiting outside in the sunshine, much more cheerful than he had been the day before. Suzanne, called in to work at time-and-a-half, had dropped him off early. He planned to come out to our place for the rest of the day.

My first step that morning was to look for something small, personal, and in good condition that could go to Alex's little daughter, Kaitlyn, but there wasn't very much. Most of Alex's furniture and basic household items had been through my hands once before, having come from either Aunty Willie's duplex or Mildred's unit at The Rainbow. He hadn't needed to buy anything new.

Tim put the toaster oven beside the door and then stood around waiting for direction. I told him about Cricket's call the evening before.

"She asked for Guns N' Roses?" Tim repeated, looking scandalized. "You can't have that at a funeral, Mom. It wouldn't be suitable."

"But Cricket said Alex wanted it."

"Better play it quietly, then," Tim advised. However, we couldn't find *Use Your Illusion* or anything else by Guns N' Roses anywhere in Alex's apartment. Tim started packing all the other cassettes we had turned up during our search and soon two small boxes were with the toaster oven, ready to be carried downstairs.

While Tim was busy with Alex's music, I went to the living room and began wrapping each grouping of ceramic wolves in several layers of newspaper.

"These are for Alex's girlfriend," I told Tim. "I know she paid for some of them; she'd better have them back."

"She might already have the one that's missing," said Tim as he helped me carry the heavy box up two flights of stairs. We knew where Alonni lived, as well as many other details of her private life because, for the last few months, Alex had seldom talked about anybody else. Among ourselves, and, hopefully, without Alex's knowledge, the family called her "Alex's new grandma." I had learned of her existence at Tim's court appearance in October of 2001…

Those who were appearing in front of the judge were supposed to be at the courthouse by 9:30 a.m., but that morning, for the very first time in his long criminal history, Tim was missing. I joined the sheriff's lineup where the offenders waited to sign in because that was the only place to get any answers at court. I knew some of the alleged criminals—young fellows, many with an FASD, who were friends of Tim and Alex —and they had a lot of news to share while we all waited.

When it was my turn, the sheriff said, "Hi, Ruth." (You know your life is a tad unusual when the court sheriff uses your first name.)

I asked, "Have you got Tim, today?"

"Yes, he's on my list and he's late." At that point Alex arrived with a cute young thing in tow but without Tim.

"Alex, let's drive over to Tim's apartment," I suggested. "He might have slept in. If we both go, you can dash upstairs while I turn the car around. And if he isn't there, we can drive through town doing a search. Your eyes are sharper than mine."

"That's a very good idea," the sheriff said. The cute young thing, whose name turned out to be Rosalee, came along with us.

Tim was at his apartment. He had slept in and was on the verge of leaving when Alex showed up at his door. A ride downtown was very welcome.

It was a quiet drive back to the courthouse, with Alex and Rosalee whispering in the rear seat and Tim half asleep beside me. I was weak with relief. Tim could easily have been anywhere on Vancouver Island that morning; he wasn't good at remembering to sleep in the right town. A warrant for his arrest would have been the next step.

For these kinds of court dates, a personal appearance on the part of the offender, with a check mark on the sheriff's list to prove that he or she had shown up, was mandatory. But the system itself didn't have to fall in line. We had been waiting for two hours when Thao Pham, Tim's lawyer, came and told us that we might as well go home. We were only there to set a date. Thao said he would stand in when it was Tim's turn. He would get a trial date organized and phone both of us later.

But while we were waiting, and while Tim and Rosalee were visiting with friends up and down the hallway, Alex asked, "Mom? Do you think age matters for dating?"

"She's too young for you."

"It's not her. It's Alonni, her mother."

I laughed until Alex got a bit irritated. He assured me feelings had nothing to do with age. "It's what's in your heart that counts."

"So, what is her age?" I asked. Alex looked vague. He thought maybe Alonni was about thirty; he thought Rosalee was about thirteen. I suspected, since she wasn't in school, that Rosalee was probably closer to seventeen, putting her mother up around thirty-five. Alonni, I was told, worked at the grocery store where I did most of my shopping; Alex thought we had already met.

"Don't worry, Mom. I'll probably get tired of her pretty soon. My girlfriends never last very long."

True enough. Alex was appallingly fickle. My basic worry regarding this particular partnership was that he would try to switch from the mother to the daughter. My faint hope was that someday a girlfriend would decide to dump him before he dumped her. It would be very good for him.

Peter and I met Alonni several times during the next few months, and, as with all the girlfriends Alex had presented to us, we liked her. He had the knack of choosing nice girls. Alonni didn't give an impression of somebody struggling for eternal youth—no visible tattoos or body piercings, and her clothes were unremarkable. She wasn't a person who needed to stand out in a crowd. One thing I especially appreciated—under Alonni's influence, Alex had stopped drinking.

After church on Christmas morning, we received the usual last minute request—could Alex bring Alonni to the family dinner on Boxing Day? Peter and I had accepted last minute, short term, live in extras at Christmas (and at every other family function) ever since 1993 when Tim brought Flora, and Kathleen brought Adam. We had never said "No." But Alonni wasn't a live in. She had her own home and her own life, quite apart from her relationship with Alex. Not only that, there was her teenage daughter to consider.

I had a legitimate excuse. "With Aunty Willie's funeral only a month ago, Dad is still sad and he doesn't feel like having anybody extra. This year, let's just stick with close family."

In late January, Alex phoned his father, needing advice regarding a trailer for rent. They went out to see it together, at an R.V. park down by the river.

Peter thought this would be a good choice for Alex. The trailer was fully furnished, it had propane heat, the rent was low, and cats were allowed. The park managers were friendly.

'Fully furnished' was bad news, in my opinion, because Alex already had a lot of furniture. Tim was willing to take it on temporarily, but Alex said, "No way! Tim would either ruin it, lose it, or sell it." Alex would rather sell his furniture himself.

I asked Alex, "What is supposed to happen when something goes wrong and you want to leave the trailer? You'll have no furnishings for the next place." Alex was positive nothing would go wrong.

The other worry, for me, was the cost of filling the propane tank. Alex was used to his heat being part of his rent. Saving ahead for a fill was something he would never understand. However, the tank had recently been filled, spring was on the way, and likely he would be gone from there before the next winter. So, the trailer as a residence sounded at least possible until I heard more about it from Tim.

The first bit of bad news: Alex was organizing a trade with a friend—all his extra furniture in exchange for the friend's car. How could our Alex possibly put the pennies in place to keep a car on the road? What about insurance? What about repairs? He couldn't even afford gasoline, but I knew nothing would stop him from driving as long as that car would run.

The second bit of bad news: Alex was hoping to share the rental fees at the new trailer with Alonni. She had been laid off after the Christmas rush, and she was alone. Rosalee was living in Vancouver with her father. Tim asked Alex where, in such a tiny little love nest, they planned to put Rosalee when her father couldn't manage her any longer. Alex said he wanted Alonni, not Rosalee.

In the end, Alonni stayed in her own apartment, keeping the door open for Rosalee, and Alex rented the trailer, cancelled the car trade, and stored his extra furniture in his dad's workshop.

Elaine and James met Alonni at Alex's trailer, and found her pleasant, easy to get along with, and very caring of Alex. Afterwards, Elaine shared the latest chapter in our family soap opera. "Alonni has two kids; did you know that, Mom?" I didn't. "Rosalee is the younger one. Her brother is nineteen, and he lives in Ontario and he has a baby. Alex is hanging out with a *grandmother!*" James and Elaine thought Alonni was closer to forty than thirty-five.

"We all like her, but I don't understand this relationship. Alex is twenty five going on fifteen; he's a teenager!" Peter exclaimed. "We know he is always looking for a mommy, but what is Alonni looking for?"

James said, "Maybe a sonny?"

I asked, "But how could anybody at her age and stage want to spend all her free time with Alex?"

"I think she must have exceptionally low self-esteem," said Elaine.

My own personal self-esteem promptly moved up a notch. It had to be one point higher than Alonni's. I loved Alex at least as much as she did, but I sure didn't want to spend long hours with him every day.

Alex was all set to go to mass with us on a wet Sunday morning in February. His planning had included Alonni. "She wants to come, too. She was raised Catholic." Alex told me he and Alonni intended to check out all the benefits the Roman Catholic Church had to offer them, this week, and all the benefits the Baptist Church had to offer, next week.

Peter was always happy to support anything church connected. I was feeling a tad nervous, not being used to girlfriends who were also grandmothers. However, when we went to collect them, Alex was alone and too miserable to go anyplace. He and Alonni had had a big fight and she had gone home. This was the first time one of Alex's girlfriends had kept her own place and hadn't allowed him to intrude. He had moved right in with Trina (16) then with Cricket (17) and finally with Louisa (18) and they all let him do it. Alonni, being twice their age, seemed to have twice their common sense.

On the following Thursday, Alex and Alonni decided to meet me at the hospital; they were waiting after my chapel time with Mary Grace. Alex had brought along some photos of Tim and Peter, with duplicates for me to keep. It was good timing because I had pictures of James and Elaine in my purse for Alex and also a nice little black and white photo of Kaitlyn that Cricket had sent.

Alex wanted me to check out his new rash. He and Alonni—together—had taken it to be seen by a doctor. The rash was worrying Alex, not because it was painful or itchy but because it was visible.

And since we were now into March, he wanted to know what was being planned for Mom's birthday. "No gifts," I requested. The best present, for me, would be a big clean up of our woods, with the whole family hauling out dead branches and burning them. Supper could be around the fire: hot dogs, potato chips, marshmallows, beer and pop, and a birthday cake. Alex and Alonni thought that was an excellent plan. They offered to bring the birthday cake.

There was more news. Alex intended to move out of his trailer and go back to an apartment. This was not a surprise. I knew he had run into a financial problem with his R.V. park managers.

Last month his propane tank ran dry before he got his Disability cheque. He had been reminded, often enough, about the expense of propane, and when we were together he had agreed that it would be smart to turn down the heat on days when a warm sweater or an extra blanket would suffice. However, he was still parading around his trailer in shorts, undershirt, and bare feet, and it wasn't spring yet.

Unfortunately, the managers had paid for the tank to be refilled, messing up both Alex's money management and his good relationship with them. Alex appeared to understand that he had to pay the money back, but so far they hadn't received anything, and I knew they never would. Their interference had also ruined what could have been a wonderful lesson. A week of being cold (Vancouver Island cold, which seldom goes below zero, especially in March) might have taught Alex to be a lot more careful about wasting heat.

Alex told me he hoped to move to an apartment in Alonni's building.

I asked, "Are you guys planning to live together?"

"No," said Alex, regretfully.

"No!" said Alonni, firmly. She added, "I need my space."

Alex did manage to get a unit in Alonni's building. Throughout March, he was busy organizing the rest of us into doing his packing for him. We moved him to his new apartment on the first of April. Next day, he was on the phone, with more medical news.

According to the doctor, the latest antibiotic, of the several tried, had finally cleared Alex's bladder infection. But according to Alex, there was "a lot of pain" happening, and he wanted Mom to help him organize a referral to a specialist.

Along with the bladder infection, Alex's body had been fighting a nasty little sexually transmitted disease: Chlamydia. Fortunately, his latest blood work showed that it had been eliminated by one of the trial antibiotics.

But there was bad news too: Alonni had been diagnosed with Hepatitis C and Alex was to start testing for that on the following Monday. He was told he'd probably gotten it by this time, and both his doctor and the office nurse had discussed the whole thing with him, "in detail," he complained. I hoped Alonni had been included in the detail because Alex had already forgotten every single thing they told him, except that he and Alonni were not supposed to use each other's toothbrushes.

I knocked on Alonni's door and then Tim knocked again, with enthusiasm. We were about to give up and leave when we heard a small scrabbling sound. Alonni was checking through the peephole to see who was outside. Tim vanished back down the stairs as the doorknob turned.

Alonni looked terrible. Her eyes were red with heavy, black circles underneath them; her face was pale; her hair uncombed; her sweater inside out. She leaned against the doorframe and stared at me.

"I thought you might like to have Alex's wolves," I said, holding the box out toward her. She unhooked her safety chain, took my load with a hoarse "Thank you," and quickly closed the door.

Tim, as expected, was waiting on the first landing. "That was short."

"I hope we did the right thing," I said. "You should have seen her; she looked awful. And she was already dressed, so we didn't get her out of bed."

"We all look awful, Mom. You look sick and so does Suzanne." We could always count on Tim for a reality check.

"As long as Alonni isn't blaming herself for Alex's death," I went on uneasily. "If you get a chance to talk to her, can you tell her what Sherry said? That it was an accident? You know her better than I do."

The trip upstairs had left us feeling unsettled. Although it was early in the day, and very little had been accomplished in the way of sorting and packing Alex's possessions, we were both more than ready to leave the apartment.

"At least we made a start," I said. "Let's stop at the church and have a quick look at the basement sound system. Maybe we can play Alex's music downstairs, during the reception. If we are allowed to have a reception."

"And if we can find the music," Tim reminded me.

Back Burning

Our coroner called late on Sunday morning, sounding worn out but also quietly triumphant, to tell us the Big House meetings were finished at last. We could go ahead with our plans for Alex's funeral and reception.

The Family had finally agreed to bury Alex at St. Paul's in Alderlea, as long as they could have a full burial, a viewing, and a traditional ceremony immediately following the funeral. Alex would be buried one space to the right of his birth mother in the row directly beyond hers. Generations' hearse would transport Alex from St. Cecelia's church to St. Paul's graveyard, and The Family would provide six pallbearers to carry him over the grass to his grave. One of St. Paul's lay leaders would be the elder in charge of the burial.

The Family had already established some ground rules: Zan and Tim, Alex's brothers, could be pallbearers only at St. Cecelia's church. Peter and I, Alex's mom and dad, were not to go to the graveyard at all. There was also a request—The Family wanted to hold a vigil at the church the night before the funeral.

"I'm not happy about that," observed Sherry, "but I promised to mention it to you."

"It's not up to us. That's Father Joe's department," I answered. "And he already said he didn't want a prayer service for security reasons. They can ask him, of course, but I doubt if he'll change his mind."

"Security is my concern as well. I've just released Alex—again—and I don't want him to be anywhere except at Generations until the funeral. I'm going to keep his police protection in place."

"I gather we aren't out of the woods yet?"

"No, we're not, but at least nobody is hiding behind any trees," said Sherry. Most were comfortable with the decisions that had been made, but the anger of the birth family's political arm was evident. They weren't a bit pleased that the final resolutions regarding Alex had gone against them and they didn't care who knew it. Sherry thought they wouldn't do anything illegal, but she wasn't taking any chances, either.

"I'm going home now. They're working out the details. They don't need me for that," she continued wearily. "I've told them they're to phone me, not you, if they need clarification."

Peter and Tim, coming in for lunch, caught the tail end of Sherry's call and reacted typically to her news.

"Alex is allowed to have a funeral," I announced.

"Good. Let's eat." Tim was a big man. I was glad his appetite had returned.

"I wonder what they'll want next," Peter said, pessimistically. He sounded almost as tired as Sherry.

A good portion of my afternoon went to phoning the friends who had promised to help at Alex's funeral. It was a sunny Sunday and people were outside enjoying the beautiful late spring weather. For the most part, I talked to answering machines. Those calls were short, easy, and undemanding.

"Hi. This is Ruth. We are allowed to have the funeral for Alex. See you on Tuesday morning."

Remembering that we could now make plans for the reception, I also left a message for Anita, head of the Compassion Committee, asking her to call back.

But connecting with Mary Grace required careful planning. She had been gone since Thursday evening; she knew nothing of all the stress and anxiety The Family had caused. It would be easier for me to talk to her tomorrow if she already had some idea of what had happened over the last four days. Since I was noticing an emotion—embarrassment—connected with my single comment of the day before, today's message to her answering machine was scribbled on scrap paper, re-grouped, then carefully re-written so that it could be read aloud without any hesitations or mistakes.

My written summarization finished with: "One reason for this call is to ask you to please sit with us at the funeral," but then, instead of stopping, I heard my voice adding, "I really need you to be there."

Where had that come from? I hadn't *felt* any need.

It was a perfect day for gardening, and our flower circle was crying out for attention, but I preferred the calm and quiet of my poorly lit office to the glorious sunshine and noisy bird song outside. Besides, this was a good time to send an email to Cricket.

> Hi, Cricket.
> First off, I want to thank you for all your funny messages. You have been giving me lots of 'up' moments at a 'down' time.
> Alex's funeral will be on Tuesday morning at St. Cecelia's Church in Alderlea. (That's the big church where we took Kaitlyn and she cried the moment the organ started to play.)
> There are some of Alex's things here that I would like Kaitlyn to have: school and Scout awards that he was proud of, a few books and pictures he valued, toys I saved from when he was small, and other little things that Kaitlyn might treasure when she is an adult. I can send them by snail mail, or if you would rather not deal with them right now, I'm happy to keep them here until a later date.
> Tim and I have been trying to find the Guns N' Roses music. So far we have been unlucky. There were no Guns N' Roses albums at Alex's place.
> The sound system at the church is very complicated for amateurs like us. I can probably find somebody who knows how to make it work or we might be able to use a ghetto blaster—if we can find the right cassette. Anyway, we will keep on trying.
> Love, Ruth

My office, with its north facing window, was cool and peaceful. I decided to take the phone off the hook and bring my journal up to date…

Most people, I'd found, didn't know what to say about Alex's death. And it was hard for me to listen while they struggled to find the right words. Sometimes I answered too fast. When they said, "We were so sorry to hear about Alex," I said, "Us, too!" Sometimes I could hardly answer at all; the words wouldn't come. Part of my problem (and this was new) was an urge to stop and argue.

Alex is at peace now implied that he hadn't been at peace before, and he might have been. How could anybody know?

No more turmoil…But Alex welcomed any turmoil that involved him and made him feel important. He enjoyed emotional upheaval.

He's in a better place…But Alex liked *this* place.

It's part of God's plan…Not! God didn't do this to us.

Probably it was a good thing for all concerned that I usually couldn't get hold of quick answers. The people who spoke to Peter got a much more conventional and courteous response.

Friends who didn't need to say anything—and who didn't need me to say anything—were the easiest to meet. They gave me a hug with no words and that said everything.

It was all reminding me of the first time Tim went to jail. The Youth Correctional System was outside the experience of our extended family and most of our friends. Except for a few women who were good at the silent hug, no one knew what to do or say and so they simply avoided the issue. As a result, I had felt terribly isolated. Apparently it was easier for people to cope with a dead son than a jailed son. Death was more familiar; most folks—at least in the over thirty crowd—had already experienced the death of a loved one.

And many of the people who knew Alex were quickly forgetting their irritation regarding his unusual FASD behaviours and were instead remembering only his good points. Some of them were turning him into a saint. That wouldn't happen for me, at least not while I was still sorting all his papers.

Anybody who truly intended to die would have gone through his boxes and shelves and drawers first and made a few trips down to the dumpster to get rid of anything confidential. (If I was given a terminal diagnosis, I'd clear my hard drive the same day and start shredding paper.) But Alex, if he had given the matter any thought at all, would probably have planned to sort and destroy his private papers after the main event.

He loved to send sentimental greeting cards for Christmas, St. Valentine's Day, Easter, Thanksgiving, Mother's Day, Father's Day, and all the family birthdays. His written comments on the cards were always the same few phrases, over and over, year after year. He didn't copy from before—he stayed with what he knew—and he invariably signed his full name.

"Happy Birthday to my wonderful Mom.

From your loving son Alex Spencer."

Last year, as assistant secretary for the society, he was made responsible for the "Thank you" cards that had to be sent out to folks who donated money. Although the reasons for the donations were different, and the amounts were different, Alex's responses to all were exactly alike.

I was finding the same duplication of phrases and repeats of thoughts and ideas in a pile of unsent love letters he left behind. The only thing that changed was the name of the girl.

———•♦•———

Sherry called again, a few moments before supper.

"Sherry! You're supposed to be resting," I exclaimed.

"They let me have a good sleep before they phoned. I'm feeling much better," said Sherry. "And there aren't any more problems. The Family wanted to let you know that they will be having a reception at the Friendship Centre after the burial, and everybody is welcome."

"Very nice of them to invite all of us, under the circumstances," I commended. "We will be having a reception at St. Cecelia's as well, and that's also open to everyone. They'll be announcing it at the end of the funeral."

"If all the people who were at the Big House meetings stay until

Tuesday, it makes sense to have two receptions," was Sherry's opinion and Anita agreed with her.

"We already knew the numbers were going to be complicated," she reminded me, "and when there is a burial right after a funeral you never know how many people will come back for coffee. Now that we know the First Nation's folks will be having their own event, we can plan for a much smaller reception."

Friends and family had been dropping in at our place over the last few days. The women brought baking, chatted with me for a few moments, and hugged Peter. The men visited with Peter, shook my hand awkwardly, and seemed happy to leave. But on Sunday, the people who belonged to our prayer group arrived unexpectedly. They all turned up together, in several vehicles, and they came for one reason—to show Peter and me that we were loved and supported. These were friends we had known and prayed with for more than twenty years. Their children had grown up with our children and they knew about our successes and failures, our disappointments and occasional triumphs, and all our public disasters. Our grief was their grief.

They brought three different kinds of cookies and stayed to eat them. We sat around the patio picnic table during the long spring twilight, drinking last summer's apple juice and Peter's homemade beer. We shared and enjoyed memories of all our children, including Alex, while the sun sank slowly behind the firs.

When they left, I said to Peter, "That was Alex's prayer service."

Another Little Bonfire

Peter and I had been sleeping badly ever since Constable Gustafsson's visit. Small aches and pains we wouldn't normally have noticed kept us awake and when we finally slept, we tossed and turned, disturbing each other all night long. Peter was blessed with my returning sleep apnea on top of his own nightmares. We were both considering asking our respective doctors for sleeping pills.

As the alarm clock began to ring on Monday morning, I said, "Good. We can finally get up," and Peter said, "Thank God that's over!"

Another day stretched ahead, with only Mary Grace's visit to look forward to. While Peter and I were eating a late breakfast, Stanley called from the Generations office. Alex's death certificate had arrived; if we wanted it today, we could pick it up any time before noon. Otherwise, they were open all day tomorrow.

I was surprised to be hearing from Stanley on a statutory holiday and uninterested in making a trip to town for that one thing, but then Stanley added, "The little service folders are here, too, and they turned out very well. It's an excellent picture of Alex."

My mother was paying for those folders. We thought she would like to see one before the funeral. We drove down into Alderlea, taking our regular route past Tzouhalem Big House with its now nearly deserted parking lot. At Generations, we paid the mandatory $27 for Alex's death certificate and then Stanley opened the package of service folders.

There, centred inside a neat oval, was Alex's teenage face with its mischievous grin and sparkling black eyes.

I took one quick look. "Well, that's the end, isn't it? That's what's left of Alex—a cute little picture and a twenty seven dollar death certificate."

Stanley handed us two or three folders to take home, but I couldn't bring myself to touch them. Peter took them and tucked them into his shirt pocket. He had tears in his eyes.

Mary Grace's visit had been planned for the early afternoon. Since dogs made her nervous, and our three were extra large, Peter put them in the basement right after lunch. They must have settled down very cozily; we were surprised to hear our outside bell ringing without their usual raucous warning. I hurried to the door, expecting Mary Grace, but the visitor was a young First Nations fellow. My heart sank. Peter looked anything but welcoming.

The stranger said, "Hi, Ruth. Hi, Peter. Don't you know me? I'm Richard Wilson." I immediately remembered the name and the connection, but it had been more than ten years and I never would have recognized the face.

I said, "Hi, Richard," and turned to Peter. "You remember Lori and Solly? This is their older brother." Seeing his blank look, I quickly added, "His dad is a carpenter; he's the one who made our picnic table."

"He still makes them," reported Richard cheerfully. He came in without further invitation, shook our hands, and made himself comfortable in Peter's favourite chair. Peter had placed him, by that time, and was asking about the carpentry business. I went to the kitchen for tea and cookies, my mind full of memories, not of Richard but of his younger brother and sister...

We had first met Rick and Evelyn Wilson at a St. Paul's Church function, to which St. Cecelia's parishioners had been invited. Their children, Nancy and this Richard, matched the ages of our oldest two; their Lori was then a tiny baby.

When Lori was two and a half, little Solly eighteen months, and

Richard and Nancy scarcely into their teens, their parents required some family counselling, and it was decided by all that a rest from the two little ones might help the whole situation. Somebody suggested calling on Peter and Ruth. "They won't mind; they always have a house full of extras."

We knew the family and so agreed to take Lori and Solly for a few days, giving their mom and dad time to regroup. After that, we had them often. We always said, "Yes." The children, both younger than Alex, were well behaved and our own kids enjoyed having them around. We knew that our support was helping the whole Wilson family.

The Wilsons lived on the other side of the highway in the catchment area for Sorrell Elementary School. Richard and Nancy, the older pair, had gone to Sorrell, but the two younger ones were enrolled in Lomas Elementary, which was outside their own district but only two houses away from our place.

Many families found the kindergarten year difficult. Kindergarten was only half a day, which meant the school bus wasn't an option. Whether a child was in morning or afternoon class, the parent who was doing the driving had a broken up day. Even for stable families, this could be tricky to manage, week after week.

The year Lori was in kindergarten, she had, according to her father, "picked up some attitude from the other children." As a result of this new assertiveness, she and her mother weren't getting along. We had Lori for two weeks during the winter while her home situation calmed.

The next year when Solly was old enough to start kindergarten, his parents asked us if we would take him for daycare. His dad would drop him off at 7 o'clock, on the way to work and pick him up in the late afternoon, on the way home. Evelyn and Rick, who were on a low income, had been able to access the government childcare subsidy of $90 a month. For the first time in the shared history of our two families, money would change hands.

Every school day, Solly arrived at 7, just in time to eat a second breakfast with my children. For the first half of the year, Alex, Tim, and Zan, who attended Lomas School, took him over to the morning kindergarten and brought him back with them at lunchtime. For the second half of the year, Solly spent his mornings with me and went to afternoon school when the boys went back after lunch. His dad was supposed to pick him up before supper but often enough Solly ate his evening meal with us and sometimes if Rick still hadn't come, I popped him into one of our extra beds for the night. On those occasions, Rick would come for Solly during the late afternoon of the second day.

We didn't know the two older Wilson kids well. James had shared some middle school classes with Nancy—he claimed she was a fantastic cook. Once, Richard and his father had borrowed our little trailer for a hunting trip.

And now, here was Richard, making himself at home in our living room. I wondered why he had come. When I asked him if he had heard our bad news about Alex, he said yes, but he didn't elaborate except to tell us that Alex and his little brother, Solly, had been special friends.

I corrected, "That was Tim, not Alex. Tim and Solly used to play street hockey together."

"Our family will be digging the grave," said Richard suddenly. "We have always been in charge of the burials and releasing the spirits. No one else is allowed to do it. I'll be helping," he added importantly, "because I'm the oldest grandson," and with that, Richard turned the conversation back toward himself and his own issues. Self, we quickly discovered, was Richard's favourite topic.

As he ate a peanut butter cookie, he let us know how much he loved peanut butter. When he moved on to the chocolate chip cookies, he listed his favourite chocolate desserts. Desserts reminded him that he was now doing his own cooking and he told us all about his new apartment.

Peter asked, "Speaking of new apartments, where are you working now?" I had to hide a grin but satire was wasted on Richard; he was delighted with Peter's interest. He worked for a contractor, he told us. He was the best man on the team and he had built every dirt track between Alderlea and Comox.

Eventually, I interrupted the monologue to ask how Lori was doing.

"She's busy, that girl," said Richard. "She has three children. She doesn't know when to stop." Poor little Lori, I thought, but prudently didn't say. What a burden for somebody barely out of her teens.

"And Solly?"

"He's doing upgrading at Malaspina College."

Richard was already back on track, giving Peter a blow by blow description of all the intricate, specialized engine work he was doing on his car. He wasn't talking about the old bucket of bolts now parked in our driveway, which looked as though nobody had ever done any work on it, specialized or otherwise. Richard and his cousin shared the ownership of a "nearly new convertible," which Richard was reconditioning in his spare time. Peter listened with more interest than I could scrape up and asked a few knowledgeable questions.

Our dogs were still in the basement, and more alert than usual because of the extra voice upstairs. Their sudden clamour told us Mary Grace had arrived, almost before her little blue car turned in at the top of the driveway. I went outside to meet her, glad of an excuse to get away from the living room.

"Do you have a visitor?" she asked, indicating the bucket of bolts.

"Do we ever," I said irritably. Usually I had almost unlimited patience with all the Richards in my life but today my tolerance had unexpectedly vanished. However, I was already feeling guilty about leaving Peter to cope with this Richard, all on his own. "Come in and meet him, then we can escape and go for a walk."

Rick Wilson had set a good example—Richard stood up and shook hands with Mary Grace as Peter introduced them.

"Mary Grace and I are going out for a walk. And Peter," giving him a meaningful look, "don't forget you have to leave in about twenty minutes." He wasn't going anywhere, but I knew my comment would help to send Richard on his way.

It was another beautiful day, sunny and warm, with a bank of clouds slowly moving in from the west. Mary Grace and I set off up the shady hill at a brisk pace, which slowed when we got out into the bright sunlight.

"So, tell me who Richard Wilson is, but first tell me how he managed to upset you," Mary Grace directed, knowing from previous experience that she had to catch the moment. Even at the best of times, my feelings were short lived.

"I don't know...Richard didn't say anything unpleasant. He didn't even say why he came. There was no reason for me to be aggravated."

"Well, feeling aggravated is better than feeling nothing," said Mary Grace. "Good for Richard. Where do you know him from?"

I shared the Spencer/Wilson connection and then answered her questions concerning the events of the last few days.

"So much trouble and distress and two families traumatized," said Mary Grace, "and you know who would have really enjoyed all this drama? Alex. It would have made him feel so important."

At that moment we were joined by a panting, tail wagging Duke, certain of his welcome. Peter had opened the basement door, and, like Mary Grace and me, Duke had escaped. He was our recently acquired black lab, a stray up until a few months before and still a wanderer.

Our other two dogs, Duchess and BooBoo, were too old to be interested in wandering. Duchess was a shepherd cross who had come to us nine years ago via a newspaper ad, "Free to a good home." Alex loved Duchess, and I knew she was going to miss his visits. BooBoo, a long, skinny schmoodle hound, had been Willie's dog and had joined our family the previous November after Willie died. Both BooBoo and Duchess stayed in their own yard unless they knew themselves to be securely leashed to their humans.

"Oh, you dog," I sighed at Duke. He sniffed Mary Grace's outstretched hand and gave her fingers a lick of acceptance. We decided to let him stay with us; it was either that or take him back and we both wanted to go on.

Mary Grace had almost memorized my phone message of the day before and now she said, "Ruth, about the funeral. I can sit close to you and Peter, but not right beside you. That's where Zan and Tim will want to be."

I said, "As long as you're close."

"I will be," Mary Grace reassured. "It's a working day; I won't be able to get away from the hospital until the last moment. Ask somebody to save me a seat in the family section."

We walked in comfortable silence for a moment until Mary Grace asked, "What are you going to wear, tomorrow?" and I immediately became a lot less comfortable. Clothes were always a headache.

"I don't know," I said. "My long black skirt doesn't fit me right now."

The almost instant weight changes that went along with disordered eating meant having to store clothes in several different sizes. Extremes at either end of the spectrum were marked Too Small to be Healthy and Why Am I Keeping These? In between were other, larger boxes identified as Small, Medium, and Might Fit Someday. These days the Medium boxes were usually sitting empty on the shelf and their contents were in my closet, a very good sign. But yesterday when I had tried on my black skirt, it had been uncomfortably loose.

"Your mother of the groom dress should fit," said Mary Grace.

My mother of the groom dress had been bought last year for James's and Elaine's wedding party. I had needed something new for the big event but had found myself anxious at the thought of shopping alone. (Buying clothes with Peter was impossible. He figured ten minutes was more than enough time to buy anything. He became disgruntled if I didn't like the garments he chose. He couldn't see any reason for a fitting room.) Mary Grace had offered her help. She and I had gone to town together and we had found the perfect dress—ideal for a wedding reception and useful for other semi-formal events as well. But I hadn't expected to wear it to a funeral.

"Mother of the groom—mother of the corpse," I murmured.

"Oh, Ruth!" groaned Mary Grace.

"Sorry. But that was supposed to be a fun dress. If I wear it for Alex, will I ever want to wear it again?"

"I think so," said Mary Grace. "There are lots of good memories already tied up in that dress and it looks nice on you and everybody likes it. Well, everybody except your mother," she added. We both laughed.

My mother was very outspoken. I had stopped at her little place immediately after buying the dress and had taken it out of its carrier bag to show her. Mom had given it a dour look. "Why did you buy purple?" she asked. "You know I hate it."

"I'm glad you can still laugh," Mary Grace commented. At the beginning of my stress disorder, my laughter, like my appetite, had vanished. It had taken a long, long time to come back, and the returning laughter was silent. Only in the last year had I been able to laugh out loud.

"You know what seems odd?" I asked. "I'm coping way better now, with Alex's death, than I did with Tim's first few times in court and in jail. Not that this is about me," I added hastily.

"Yes it is; I'm here for you," said Mary Grace. "And I think one difference is that you have Peter's support now, and you didn't have it when Tim hit the system."

I nodded. We had both grown a lot since those days. Peter, finally understanding that Tim was brain damaged rather than 'bad,' had stopped trying to protect his reputation and I had learned how to be interdependent instead of codependent.

We stopped at the next corner, wondering if we should go on or if it was time to go back. Duke made the decision for us; he stretched, scratched himself, and started homeward. We followed along slowly, with Mary Grace continuing her train of thought.

"Grief is very complicated and it's different for all of us," she said gently. "You probably haven't even started the process, considering everything else that's going on. And you know, Ruth, it hasn't been easy being Alex's mother, these last few years. I think you have already done some of your grieving for him."

This was warm, comforting wisdom; it spread through my body and relaxed some of the tension in my stomach.

"Thank you," I said. "That makes me feel a whole lot more normal. Some of my reactions have seemed a bit off centre."

"Can you tell me?"

"Well, for one thing, Father Joe gave us a mini lecture on the church's changed position regarding suicide. He thought he ought to reassure us." Peter and Zan had listened courteously, but I had tuned Joe out, the way I had blocked the voices of my maths teachers during high school. I already knew Alex was with God. The official

Roman Catholic stance, past or present, didn't interest me.

"I should have paid attention, though," I said contritely. "Joe was trying to help."

"Don't beat yourself up over it. He could have asked for your opinion instead of offering his. What else?"

"Sara's letters," I said. "They almost made me start crying."

"But Ruth, that's not an unusual response. You've lost your youngest son. It's okay to feel sad about it."

"Well, I didn't remember that feeling. And I was afraid of starting to cry because what if I couldn't stop?"

"Crying is natural; it isn't something to be afraid of and it does stop," said Mary Grace. "I think this is the closest to tears that you have ever been. Your Sara must be a very good writer."

"She is," I confirmed.

"Why don't you bring her letters when you come to see me on Thursday," Mary Grace suggested. "We can read them together. The chapel is a safe place for crying." I didn't agree. Crying and the emotions that might go along with it seemed totally *un*safe, even in the chapel.

"Anything else you need to tell me?" asked Mary Grace.

"Yes." But this was harder and I needed a moment to organize my thoughts. "It's not only the First Nations folks who think we should hand Alex over to his birth family," I explained carefully. "Other people are saying, 'You have all the memories. Why can't you let them have the body?'"

"They actually said that?"

"Yes. One of them said it was a good way to thank the birth family for 'the gift of Alex.' And somebody else said, 'It's the right thing to do.'"

"It's not; it's ridiculous," said Mary Grace flatly. "Do the people who feel that way have any children of their own?"

"My cousin has her son for school holidays. I asked her, 'Would you let strangers take Charlie away if he died?' and she said, 'That's different. Charlie isn't adopted.'"

"Do *you* think there is a difference?" Mary Grace asked.

"Of course not—not in the way my cousin meant. If James died,

Elaine would be in charge of everything and her family would be supporting her and some of them would be strangers to me, and that would be okay. But it wouldn't be okay if Zan or Tim or Kathleen died and people I didn't know wanted their bodies—and that has nothing to do with adoption."

"That's what counts," said Mary Grace. "You can't do anything about the ignorance of people who don't understand, but you can know what is right for you…and for Alex."

"I do know what's right for Alex."

"Well?"

"Alex would want his mom and dad to take care of him. And I don't know why I didn't sort that out for myself."

"It's easy to get confused when you're dealing with something this big," Mary Grace comforted. For the rest of the walk back, she told me about her own weekend instead of asking about mine. She knew I could relax when I was doing the listening.

"Are you feeling better?" she asked as we turned off the road into our shadowy driveway. Duke started to run down the hill; his water bowl was calling to him. I stopped in the coolness.

"Sometimes I feel as if I'm just going through the motions and nothing is real," I said. Mary Grace nodded. "And sometimes it's like I'm standing back, watching myself doing dishes or talking to other people. It feels like I'm outside myself." She nodded again. "And sometimes it's a roller coaster ride—up and down so fast I can't keep track of it all." I smiled at Mary Grace as we moved on. "But right now, I think I'm feeling peaceful."

The peaceful feeling lasted until we got back to the house, where we found Peter making more tea.

"I saw you coming; it'll be ready in a moment," he sang out from the kitchen as we opened the front door.

Richard had finished off the cookies before he left. I washed my hands, took a package of little homemade butter tarts from the freezer, and spread them out on a plate to defrost, wondering absentmindedly who had brought them and hoping I had thanked the donor.

Mary Grace asked, "Did Richard ever say why he came?"

"He wanted a picture of Alex," said Peter.

"Why would he want that?"

"He said The Family were having some booklets made up to hand out at the church. They wanted a snapshot of Alex for the front page."

"Did you give him one?" I asked apprehensively.

"Of course not," said Peter. "I told him it wasn't up to me. They aren't my pictures. I said, 'You'll have to ask Ruth for that.'"

"Pictures of Alex are precious," I said, "and I'm not giving them to anybody. What if he forgot to bring it back?"

"The Family must have taken some photos of Alex for themselves. He's been up to Campbell River often enough," Mary Grace pointed out.

Peter shrugged. "Richard wasn't upset when I said 'No.' I don't think he cared one way or the other. The Family sent him to ask, so he asked."

"Yes, but *we* are supposed to be doing the church piece." I was getting anxious. "They are supposed to be doing the graveyard piece. That's what Sherry said yesterday. They can't suddenly start changing everything around."

"Don't worry, it's only folders," said Mary Grace soothingly. "They probably won't be able to find a printer willing to work on a holiday. And tomorrow morning the ushers from Generations will be at the back of the church, keeping an eye on things. If The Family is there with handouts, they can be asked to give them out at the graveyard, instead."

Tim and Suzanne had promised to spend some of the day searching for the missing Guns N' Roses music. Tim phoned after supper.

"We couldn't find Alex's cassettes, Mom. I knew Frankie didn't borrow them; he hates Guns N' Roses. We asked a few other people, but nobody knew anything."

"Did you try Alex's girlfriend?"

"We went up," said Tim. "She wasn't home. Did you talk to Cricket?"

"She called a few moments ago. She said all the music stores in Calgary were closed for the long weekend. They were closed here, too. Dad and I even went to the supermarkets, but they didn't have anything by Guns N' Roses."

"Too bad," said Tim.

"Well, we tried," I said, "and that's all we can do. Alex would understand."

As usual, my day finished in front of the computer. Also as usual, my last email, pulling the day together, went to Zan.

> Hi Zan.
>
> Kathleen is calling every day, usually at suppertime. I'm glad she's keeping in touch with us because Joseph isn't very supportive. She said she appreciated your phone call.
>
> Tim is doing better now that things are a bit more settled. Quite weepy, but at least he has started eating again. Today he said, "If we were a native family those Indians couldn't care less about Alex. It's only because we are a white family that they are making such a big deal out of it." He's right although we could hardly be called a 'white' family when half of us are First Nations! (It's funny that Dad and I always say "First Nations" but Tim, who is First Nations, always says "those Indians." And Stanley from the Funeral Parlour, who is also First Nations, says "the Natives.") I admire the way Tim is so settled, inside himself, with regard to his heritage. He is like a giant with one leg on either side of the great divide and a foot firmly placed in both camps. And he is friends with everybody. Alex was always more of an 'apple'—red on the outside, white on the inside, even after his birth relatives got involved in his life.
>
> Do you remember Anita? She taught Alex in kindergarten and now she's in charge of the food for his funeral reception. She said all the members of our prayer group phoned her, separately, and offered to help make the sandwiches early tomorrow morning. Loads of other people also wanted to help and they will

all be baking sweet stuff at home and bringing it ready to serve.

The First Nations people are in charge of the graveyard service and they will be providing their own pallbearers for that, so you and Tim won't be needed there, only at St. Cecelia's. Dad and I have been asked to stay away from the graveyard. We will be drinking coffee and eating a million miles of sandwiches in St. Cecelia's basement while Alex is being buried. But everybody else can choose to go because cemeteries aren't private. Tim is planning to be there. (I asked Stanley to keep an eye on him.) Sherry, our coroner, will be going and Mary Grace will be supporting her. I hope Clare will be staying at St. Cecelia's with me.

Alex's birth family wants to bury him with that big, expensive, solid silver ring they gave him when his birth father died—the one he kept on the chain around his neck, always. Unfortunately, that ring is still missing.

We had a nice day but a windy evening, and now the sky is full of those little clouds Dad calls "schoppkens groppkens." It's the end of the good weather. I bet we get rain tomorrow.

Love, Mom

Beacon of Hope

Long ago I had made an arrangement with the Finance Committee at St. Cecelia's—minimum wage to be paid to the janitor in exchange for free use of the church copier. It was a fair bargain. As well as my own things, I often had a lot of FASD copying to do and the charge in town was 25 cents a page. For their part, the church financial people were getting a team of dedicated, professional custodians at the lowest possible rate.

When our church office opened at 8:30 a.m. on Tuesday morning, I was already outside waiting. The two unfamiliar hymns Peter and I wanted for Alex's funeral, 'Brother James' Air' and "Jesus Loves Me," were both typed on one page ready for copying. I also planned to do seventy-five copies of Alex's life story[3], already published by SNAP Magazine as 'Alex's Story.'[4]

Alex's Story

My life started on October 20, 1976 in Campbell River, B.C. I stayed with my birth family till I was 18 months at which time I was brought into a loving foster home. This wonderful and caring family kept me for six months after which time the court ruled that I could stay for another six months. I was well

---

3   Original spelling and grammar of Alex's story retained

4   First published as "Alex's Story." *SNAP Newsmagazine* January 2002.

taken care of and loved by my foster parents and three older brothers and older sister and other foster kids that came for short stays. When my six months was up the court ruled again that I could stay for another six months. With this ruling I became a permanent ward. I loved being there and they loved having me. I played with my sibblings all the time and let's say things couldn't be better.

But then my bilogical uncle and aunt wanted to adopt me. At this time I was four years old and I was used to this loving family and did not remember my bilogical family at all. So visits were planned, but I refused to go. My uncle and aunt tried to talk me into it, but I wouldn't move. This led them to canceling their adoption application. But we stayed in contact with cards, letters and photographs. When I was 9 my foster parents finished the adoption papers and I could be theirs and everyone was happy.

I was about 17 years of age when my uncle and aunt resurfaced with cousins around my age so visits were planned again. I got to meet all my family which was a very big family. During this time I would visit them on a regular basis and tell my adopted family all the good times I had which hurt them which at that time I didn't understand but now I do. They loved me and thought of me as theirs and I was going to my other family. This now makes sense to me and I kind of betrayed them, but they still love me and I love them. In closing this part of my life I must apolagize for any pain I inflicted upon their good name or feelings.

In the next part of my life story I will explain about my schooling. I was let's say a slow learner and did kindergarten twice and the rest of my elementary years were let's say harder than the average student. I had to have homework notes that my mother had to ask for as soon as I got home or I would lose them or forget to do my homework. My mom was always behind me to do my homework or chores before I got to play with my brothers and friends which I found annoying then, but now I'm glad. I did especially well with teachers that spent a long time with me and of course my mom being behind me at home to support me. Having less distractions visually and less students in class also helped me. So my advice would be to have good home support, teachers/aids, smaller classes and visual aids and homework notes and a good filing system at home to keep reports and asignments in for future refference.

Getting along with other students wasn't really hard for me in school.

I always had good friends that would help me when needed and never did pick on me for being a slow learner. I think it is important no one gets picked on in school and being involved in extra sports and band activities. I spent six years in band class and five years in track and field cross country running which I thoroughly enjoyed and was good at. Everyone seemed to enjoy my team approach and sense of humour which I have lost over the years to some extent.

Next I will share my involvement in community activities such as air cadets, boy scouts, altar serving, and summer camps. Ever since I was five I have been involved in community organizations. All were enjoyed by me and I learned a lot, especially team work and serving my community in many ways which I am very proud of. I actually won an award one year for doing volunteer work through the scout program. It felt really good to be recognized. For the last two years I have been involved in my community by doing education about Fetal Alcohol Syndrome and helping out in other ways to make our community "FASD Friendly" which it wasn't when I was growing up. I can happily say now it is changing thanks to my mom and other wonderful concerned people. A big thank you to all of them. I really enjoy doing this kind of work and my hope is to make life easier for anyone with FASD and their families by sharing my life experiences. Some paid work for myself would be nice, but I think it is more important that people learn about FASD and be supportive of those living with it so they can achieve their greatest potential in life. It takes time and patience but is definitely worth it in the long run. At this time I would like to thank my family especially my parents for doing a really good job for keeping me busy and giving me tools to deal with my past, present and future.

Family life is my next topic. I grew up in a small community with lots of family time. We have a family that has stayed close through good and bad times. Each time one of us would go through a rough time we could count on others in the family to support us. We all know that we would all be there if we could and even the distance couldn't stop us from contact through the phone, letters and emails. We all appreciate the times when we are together again. As a family we all took part in family chores which included raising animals as well as our own vegtables. Plus we helped with grocery shopping and household chores. We learned a lot so thanks mom and dad.

In July, 1998 I became a dad to Kaitlyn which means a lot to me and always will even though distance is a barrier to our relationship at this point. I still stay in contact with Kaitlyn's mom via mail, phone and email which the rest of my family does as well.

In closing I would like to thank everyone that has touched and helped my life become the way it is now.

Alex Spencer

The first section of Alex's story—everything before his seventeenth birthday—had been poorly plagiarized from some of my earlier work. The rest was his own. I was proud of the way he had pulled his half forgotten memories together, but now some of his words were hard for me to read. For his birth family, other bits might be even harder.

I didn't want Alex's immediate birth family to be hurt. Aunty Loretta, Aunty Rhonda, Uncle Edward, Aunty Sandra, and Alex's grandmother had already gone the extra mile; for their sake, Peter and I had changed our original plan to hand out the life story at the funeral reception. Instead, we had decided to make a few copies and share them with any friends we happened to be in contact with over the next few weeks. But now, with two receptions happening, we were going back to Plan A. All the people who came to the funeral reception at St. Cecelia's could, if they wished, take home a copy of the life story.

My song sheets, hot off the press, were placed on the table in the church lobby ready for Della to hand out, but the copies of Alex's life story couldn't be left there. The best place for those was downstairs in the locked janitor's room, next door to the hall, where they would be out of sight during the funeral and easy to retrieve at the reception. I needed to go downstairs, anyway.

Ordinarily I cleaned St. Cecelia's hall on Monday mornings but yesterday my job had been the furthest thing from my mind. Since it was still early, this morning seemed a good time to at least empty the garbage cans and replace paper products in the washrooms.

The ladies making sandwiches for Alex's funeral luncheon were chatting cheerfully as I went down the stairs. They became very silent when I passed the kitchen. A few said "Hi, Ruth," but I could see that my presence was making all of them uncomfortable. It wasn't an appropriate time to be a janitor. I locked the life story into the supply cupboard and returned home, under a grey overcast sky.

There were another two hours to get through before the funeral, but Peter was pacing up and down our living room, already wearing his good jacket over a white shirt and black tie. His funeral flowers, a pot of yellow chrysanthemums given to him for his birthday the day before Alex died, were beside the door ready to go. I wondered out loud if it would be a good idea to take a big vase of columbine from our own garden, as well, and Peter jumped at the suggestion. He headed outside, clippers in hand. I went downstairs to change my clothes.

As I took the mother of the groom dress out of the closet, a small flat, earthenware heart hanging on a short ribbon bumped softly against my arm. The heart was glazed white, with a flower and the word 'hug' double glazed on the front in blue. Mary Grace had given it to me, long ago, to celebrate the first money I earned as a published poet.

Because this favourite dress had a matching jacket but no pockets, the little heart was pinned to an inside seam of the jacket where it hung out of sight, close to my hip, and could be easily grasped for courage or comfort. Most of my pockets held a small, smooth stone—substitute for a set of Greek worry beads—and most of my stones had come from Mary Grace.

Just after 10 o'clock, when I was dressed up far beyond my 'casual' comfort zone, Peter's vase was filled with pink and purple columbine along with a few incompatible red tulips the browsing deer had missed, and we were both killing time drinking cups of coffee we didn't want, Suzanne and Tim arrived at our door. We hadn't expected to see these two before the funeral. Peter, pleased to have something to do, poured two more cups of coffee and brought the last of yesterday's tarts to the table.

Tim was looking very smart in a new black shirt, a big improvement over his usual baggy hockey jerseys. He said it was a gift from Suzanne's dad, but for once he wasn't interested in his clothes. He and Suzanne had come directly from the viewing at Generations, and both were distressed.

"They came but they didn't stay," said Tim.

"Who?" I asked.

"Alex's other family. My friends came, and Alex's friends, and we stayed for the whole time but not them."

"I wanted to have a quiet time with Alex," Suzanne said miserably, "but they were so loud."

"I'm assuming we're talking about the viewing," I said, "but so far, it's hard to tell what happened."

"A few of them came," said Tim. "They walked up to the front and looked at Alex, but they didn't stay and pray." Tim hadn't stayed to pray either. He said he had looked at Alex, but then he went back outside and shook hands with people as they came in.

"I wanted to make sure nothing happened," he told us.

"Weren't the police there to do that?" asked Peter.

"Yes, all over the place, but Alex is *my* brother."

I found myself feeling sorry for The Family. They had probably expected this to be a private viewing, just for them. The police presence, a deterrent to the few hot heads, would have seemed insulting to those who had no intention of doing anything against the law. And it must have been quite a shock when they found the Generations chapel filled with Caucasian young people. Members of The Family who were fighting for Alex's rights without knowing anything about him would have been unaware of his outgoing nature, his popularity, and his many girlfriends with blond hair and blue eyes.

"Those people weren't quiet; they had no respect for Alex," said Suzanne, wiping away a tear. "One guy stomped his feet all the way in and left by the side door. And two girls looked at Alex for a while and then they started wailing."

"Those girls weren't Alex's friends," Tim put in. "I never saw them before."

"They might be family from far away," I explained. "If they had been asked to lead the mourning, then they were supposed to cry, and encourage everybody else to cry, too."

Peter asked, "Ruth, how do you know that?"

"Alex told me. Remember when his birth father died? Alex said they were all supposed to get their crying over with on the day of the funeral and the louder the better." Suzanne and Tim were paying attention, so I added, "It's another cultural thing, different than our way, but that doesn't make it wrong."

Peter stood up. "It's time to go," he said. "Better bring a coat,

Ruth—it's starting to rain."

As we were preparing to leave, Tim took me to one side.

"I'm going to take over Alex's job," he announced. Seeing my puzzlement, he elaborated. "I talked it over with Suzanne."

"Which job?" I asked. Alex had been on call at the local A&W for the last year but somehow I couldn't see Tim slinging burgers.

"All the talking and stuff he did for FASD. He was good. I won't be as good as him, but I want to keep it going so people won't forget him."

"That's a wonderful idea," I said, knowing Tim would be welcomed with open arms. He already knew all the people involved, having helped with the clearing out and painting when we first opened our street front office, and he had some basic knowledge of Alex's FASD work...

Two weeks ago, our FASD society had put on a workshop, "Strategies for Success." Members of the mentorship team, scheduled to participate in a panel discussion, had asked Tim to join them.

The mentorship panel happened at lunchtime; workshop participants were supposed to do their eating while it was going on. The panellists sat at the head table with their lunches and drinks in front of them and we had hoped they would be able to eat when it wasn't their turn to talk, but they mostly didn't eat. Before the panel started, Tim had asked me to sit with him. He took the end chair, with Mom beside him but around the corner of the table. I was happy to support Tim but being in front of the crowd meant I couldn't eat, either.

The kids on the panel did well. (They weren't actually kids—they were all well into their twenties.) Coletta was the best speaker, but Alex and George also had a lot of confidence. Alex was funny; he made everybody laugh. George made everybody nervous.

When it was Alex's turn, he first introduced himself, then turned and introduced Tim. "That big guy is my brother, Tim. He's shy, and he won't talk very much, but I talk enough for both of us." Tim didn't volunteer any information, but he did manage to answer two direct questions about the legal system and corrections.

Afterwards, several people said, "proud mom," and I was.

Margaret was equally proud of Coletta. George told the whole group how important it was to have family support. He said, "I wish my mom supported me the way Alex's and Tim's mother supports them."

Deb Evensen, a well known teacher from Alaska, was our guest speaker. She travelled all over North America teaching other teachers how to educate children with FASD. She seemed such a down home, everyday sort of person; to meet her, you would never think of her as anything out of the ordinary. And then, seemingly without effort, she would have a whole roomful of people hanging on her words.

Deb wanted all of us to understand how unusual it was to find a group of adults with FASD who were diagnosed, pulled together into a working group, and able to share their life experiences. After the panel, when we were in another study session, she said, "You can compare those four to a group of four Rhodes Scholars. They have put in just as much work to get this far." She also gave their parents and support people a lot of credit.

"The group will be absolutely delighted to have you," I told Tim.

"Are you guys ever coming?" asked Peter from the doorway.

Tim drove off with Suzanne, and Peter hustled me into the truck. What with balancing his vase of flowers on my lap, holding the pot of chrysanthemums steady between my feet, and sharing Tim's exciting news, my thoughts stayed away from Alex all the way to St. Cecelia's.

The Funeral

There were several cars in the church parking lot ahead of us. A police cruiser and Generations' funeral coach occupied the 'no parking' fire lane directly in front of the closed church doors. No activity was happening around either vehicle; Alex had already been taken inside. Remembering Stanley's comments at the funeral home last Saturday, Peter parked as close to the building as possible and locked up with care. I left the truck reluctantly, wishing I could stay right there for the next three hours.

Inside the church, we saw Alex's grey casket resting on a trolley at the far end of the lobby. Closer to the main doors, Della was putting printed song sheets inside hymnbooks and the Generations people were setting up their table, complete with a basket for cards and a stack of Alex's little funeral folders. The guest book was open and ready for signatures. I closed it, checking the cover to make sure it was the one Tim had chosen and was politely reprimanded by an usher.

The church was empty apart from Linda and Rachael going over their music up at the front and Kelsey, one of Alex's friends, crying at the back. Peter centred his flowers on the carpet before the altar, where they made a bright splash of colour, and we sat down together in the section reserved for family.

Neither Peter nor I, nor anybody else in the family, had thought of organizing a preservice meeting spot for all of us. In any case, there were only two places at St. Cecelia's where families could meet: the church coffee room, small and crowded, or the basement where, today, the ladies were still working. Our church needed a nice sitting room with direct access to the worship area—a place where grieving families could collect before a funeral and enter the church together at the last moment.

Peter didn't mind sitting at the front with his back to the door, but I quickly began to feel both exposed and threatened. These feelings of vulnerability weren't new; they had been a nasty complication of returning emotions a few years ago and continued to be troublesome on occasion. Today I suddenly needed to be on my feet facing the unknown. I also needed to be a whole lot closer to Alex. As soon as Tim and Suzanne settled themselves beside Peter, I went back to the lobby and stood at the far end with Alex directly behind me.

The congregation was beginning to arrive, First Nations mingling easily with the rest, and all were lining up together to sign the guest book. To my surprise, more than half of the nonnative folks were strangers to me. When Zan came in, I asked, "Do you know all these people?"

"Of course not," said Zan. "It's not my funeral. Where's Dad?"

Two enormous bouquets of purple lilac in home vases came through the now wide open church doors, filling the lobby with their glorious perfume. Two friends, bearers of the flowers, paused to smile at me before they moved on toward the altar. In that moment, I knew purple lilac would always bring back memories of Alex.

Several years ago, as an element of recovery from complex stress disorder, I had accepted an invitation to join a group of strong, mature women who were studying the Enneagram, a Sufi practice of self knowledge and spiritual transformation. Today, the third Tuesday of the month, was regularly our Enneagram meeting. The women must have been in touch with each other over the weekend, arranging to meet outside the church, because they all trooped in together, a confident, self possessed, older crowd. One at a time, they stepped out of the guest book queue to give me a hug.

Members of the FASD Society entered separately and were much less relaxed than the Enneagram people. For one thing, they had known Alex personally for many years; for another, they were struggling with all the "if onlys" that are the fallout of any suicide. Members of the society who were also parents now had more fears than ever for their damaged children. And they all needed to know that Peter and I were okay.

Raelene, part of our group of young people with FASD, arrived carrying her brand new baby. The baby was so new that Raelene was still an inpatient at the local hospital; she had a plastic Maternity Ward bracelet clipped around her arm. Somebody brought her to the church, and she had to go straight back to her bed as soon as the funeral was over, but the important thing, for Raelene, was that she not miss one of the emotional highlights of the year.

Tim's friend, Justin, came in flanked by two lawyers, Thao Tran and Ajeet Bannarjee. Ajeet knew Alex and me because of the many hours we spent at the courthouse supporting Tim. Court was made a little less painful for me because of Ajeet's continuing interest in FASD.

Always a bit vague due to a traumatic brain injury when he was only six years old, Justin seemed even more disoriented than usual as I hugged him and showed him where Tim and Suzanne were sitting. He moved off slowly, looking confused, and Ajeet went with him. Thao stopped to talk.

"Good morning, Ruth. Thanks for letting me know about Alex."

"You're welcome. Thanks for bringing Justin."

"The judge was willing to hold his case over as long as he was supervised," Thao explained. "We'll have to get him back in time for afternoon court."

"Well, he wouldn't have made it here on his own," I said, "and he doesn't look in good enough shape to be a pallbearer. But I truly appreciate that you brought him. Tim will be pleased."

Several elderly First Nations ladies had arrived by that time. I rummaged through my purse for the envelope of Kaitlyn's photos, left my safe corner, and went in search of Alex's birth grandmother. From the back of the church, it looked as if First Nations folks had appropriated the right hand side and all others had settled to the left, but, moving forward, I saw that there were several pockets of amalgamation.

I asked a young woman who was standing in the side aisle if she knew Alex's grandmother. She wasn't friendly, but she silently tipped her chin toward two women sitting together a few rows away. Walking across, I said to the elder of the two, "Are you Alex's Grandma?"

"Yes," she said, with a wide smile.

The woman beside her, who looked about my age, said angrily, and with emphasis, "This is *Bellman's* grandmother, and I'm his auntie."

Anger always made me tense and anxious but since I was standing, and they were still seated, it was safe to smile (cautiously) at Alex's Grandma. "I'm Ruth. I thought you might like to have some baby pictures of Kaitlyn," I said, handing her the envelope. She took it eagerly.

The other woman looked at the envelope and brusquely asked me, "Where is the girl? What's her address?"

I was afraid to look at her. Speaking directly to Alex's Grandma, and avoiding even glancing at the auntie, I said, "Kaitlyn is living in Alberta now."

It seemed odd to be both experiencing intense feelings and actually noticing them. I went back to the lobby shaking with nervous tension and wondering how on earth Mary Grace could be approving of emotions.

Ursula, a longtime friend, was standing in the guest book lineup with one of her tall sons waiting behind her. Seeing them together took my thoughts away from the present misery and back into the far past. Ursula's youngest, who was Alex's age, had been placed with us twice during his preschool years as a 'failure to thrive.' Because he had to be dropped off at home every weekend and because, like me, Ursula had a houseful of little children, our kids got acquainted. Years later I helped Ursula get government financing to send her four to the same summer camp my lot attended. As a result, Kathleen became good friends with the younger daughter and Tim was still in touch with the boys. Of all the First Nations people who came to Alex's funeral that day, Ursula was the only one who gave me a hug.

Among the last to arrive were Alice, an FASD Society member, and Oliver, her son. I was surprised to see Oliver. He and Alex were friends, but I thought he was serving time in the minimum security jail over at Maple Ridge, on the mainland.

"He is," confirmed Alice. She had managed, with a series of long distance telephone calls, to spring him for twenty four hours and she had crossed over to the mainland the night before, a four hour trip each way, just to bring him to Alex's funeral. She had to take him back to the jail that afternoon.

The parking lot had filled. Vehicles were now overflowing onto the roads around the church. Mary Grace was running late, but I knew she would find a place to leave her car. Apart from the employees of Alderlea's two funeral homes, Mary Grace attended more funerals than anybody else in town. The support and comfort she offered to those who were dying, and to their families both before and after the death, meant that she was often asked to attend, take part in, or even to lead, the funeral. She was very accomplished at finding last minute parking spots at all the local churches.

Father Joe and the cross bearer came into the lobby, both dressed in their funeral vestments. Mary Grace was right behind them. She hugged me and asked, "Where will you be sitting? Did you save a place for me?" I pointed to the left side, where Suzanne had draped a jacket over the chair directly behind her own.

"I'll go and sit down. Are you coming?"

"In a moment," I whispered.

This would be my last time with Alex and I wasn't quite ready to leave. Mary Grace slid her hand into mine and left me holding a small, smooth stone with 'peace' written on the flat surface in black Gothic script. My fingers tightened around it.

Father Joe signalled that it was time to start. The cross bearer stepped forward and stood in the doorway, ready to lead the procession. I had to move over as three Generations ushers busily surrounded Alex's casket and positioned it in the centre of the lobby right behind the cross. Vera and Allanah were standing by, all set to spread the white pall, and Alex's six pallbearers had collected.

Caskets brought to St. Cecelia's by Stanley and his staff were topped with an attractive wall crucifix, compliments of Generations. (The Protestants got a bare cross.) These ornaments weren't meant to be buried; they were intended for the family. After the funeral, they could be taken home, hung, and cherished in memory of the person who had died.

Six months ago, just before we spread the pall over Willie's casket, Father Joe had given me her crucifix. Now he removed Alex's and handed it to me. I didn't need another one. Not only that, my hand was already occupied with Mary Grace's little peace stone. Passing the crucifix on to Tim, who was delighted to receive it, I left the lobby. It didn't feel like my place anymore and now, with the church almost full, the only people who would notice me up at the front with my back to the crowd would be those sitting directly behind our family.

Peter was glad to see me. "Finally," he smiled, and took his hymn-book off my chair.

My mother the matriarch, who was very deaf, leaned forward and said in what she fondly imagined to be a whisper, "Where the hell have you been?" The whole family regressed into nervous giggles.

I had enough time for a quick look around before the service started. Filling the side section closest to us were Justin with his lawyers, Raelene holding her tiny baby, Alex's gaggle of blond girlfriends, and some untidy, rough looking guys I recognized as food bank regulars. The flowers in front of the altar, with purple lilac predominating, were exactly what Alex, the conservative, would have liked. A lot of colour, and nobody had brought anything overpowering or outlandish. To my right, a few chairs were empty although there was a row of people standing with the uniformed police at the back. I caught Clare's eye and we shared a smile as Rachael announced our first hymn, Linda's beautiful music filled the church, and the cross bearer slowly led Alex's procession up the centre aisle.

Any Roman Catholic Mass is filled with ritual and symbolism. Usually my concentration was on the words but that day, unable to pay attention, I found myself being upheld and carried along by the predictability and familiarity of the service. Nothing penetrated, apart from the general hostility in the air, until Father Joe started his homily.

The Catholic funeral homily, or sermon, was not supposed to be a eulogy. There were a few references to the person who had died but only in terms of God's love. Emphasis was placed on the power and presence of God—in scripture, in the gathered people, and in the life of the deceased. The only time I ever heard Father Joe deviate from this approved format was at Alex's funeral.

Like us, Joe could sense the tension and animosity in the church; unlike us, he could do something about it. He began his homily by first emphasizing Alex's lifelong commitment to his spiritual community, including his many years as an altar server.

He then highlighted Alex's involvement in the larger community. Twelve years of Scouting, culminating in a special service award. Three years in Air Cadets, where he earned a music credit. The junior and senior high school bands, where Alex's trumpet playing was undistinguished but his willingness to be helpful had merited a citizenship crest. As a teenager, he volunteered at the BC Winter Games and with the Canadian Red Cross. As an adult, he worked for the FASD community.

"Alex was a person who shared his skills and talents," said Father Joe, "and by doing that he enriched the lives of others."

In my opinion, this would have been the perfect place for Joe to wrap it up. Members of The Family would now understand that Alex had enjoyed a full life, quite apart from his association with them.

But Father Joe wasn't finished. "Alex belonged to two special communities where he was loved and cherished," he went on, "and he personified the best of both."

He had been born into a strong family who relied on traditional values. Joe talked about the strengths Alex had inherited from his birth family—respect for elders, care of relatives, patience, good listening skills, love of nature, generosity and sharing, a deep-seated spirituality—and the ways Alex's adoptive family had developed those principles. He repeated some of the stories Peter and Zan had told him two days before, pointing out cultural similarities and painting a picture of shared beliefs.

I realized, with surprise, that Joe was right; our family's values did match First Nations values. The generosity and sharing were certainly a good fit. Our children had spent their whole childhood generously sharing their home and their parents with strangers. Had they protested, we would have immediately stopped looking after all the extras.

Love of nature? I remembered little Alex, a three year old, bringing Mommy the first dandelions of the season. We all went for a nature appreciation walk together on Sunday afternoons, rain or shine, sometimes in our own neighbourhood, sometimes at a park or on a beach. At one time, the kids had owned a communal collection of bird nests so big that the only place to house it was under their parents' bed. Watering and weeding the vegetable garden, also euphemistically called *nature appreciation* as in "Get the hoe; it's your turn to appreciate nature," were compulsory family activities.

Peter and I were strong believers in outdoor fun. The sandbox in our backyard had stretched over time into a huge dirt pile, always covered with small, battered cars and trucks, miniature earth moving equipment and boys. We had the usual complement of swings and monkey bars, bikes and wagons, as well as a fort and an old rowboat, all vying for space among the fruit trees. A big trampoline, purchased about the time James started kindergarten and the three little ones were toddlers, provided many hours of fun for all of us. Family skipping parties were held on the driveway with the neighbourhood kids joining in. Sometimes we laughed so much we could hardly turn the ropes.

I wasn't sure what Father Joe meant with his "…deep seated spirituality." My First Nations friends described spirituality as "Knowing who I am." Mary Grace said, "Being firmly connected to your community." For Clare, it was "Having a zest for life!" and for me, "Finding God inside every disaster." But Alex's only conscious idea of spirituality, I suspected, had been "going to church." Maybe, at an unconscious level, there had been something more.

For us, and for the First Nations, extended family and nuclear family were equally important. A few days ago, James and Tim had been laughing at the way Alex took care of our elders. But it was noticeable, in our family of many boys, that Alex was always the first to step forward to meet his Grandma and the ancient aunts, receiving and hanging their coats and guiding each of them to a chair.

Father Joe talked about the difference between the First Nations ideal of friendly competition, which Alex had learned in our family and the single-minded competitiveness of Canadians in general. Zan raised a dubious eyebrow toward me at that point. Our family wasn't entirely free of the desire to win.

My children hadn't been involved in organized sports, and only Kathleen and Zan had ever cared about being on school teams, but the annual Egg Decorating Competition at Lomas Elementary, which offered a small chocolate egg for all entries and large chocolate rabbits for the winners, had caught their interest. They often brought home second and third prizes. One year James pestered his father for a square of plywood, created some plaster hills on its best surface, and sprayed the lot with bright green paint. When the paint was dry, he glued on plastic trees and a blue paper pond and placed some of his electric train track in strategic spots. His 'train' was a row of brightly dyed eggs, finishing off with a little red caboose. He won first prize in his age group. A few years later, Zan and Tim asked me to save a huge duck egg and some tiny bantam eggs for their entry. These came together on blue and green cardboard as the story of "The Ugly Duckling," winning another first for the Spencer kids.

To make the kitchen a fun place, I taught my children how to cook the things they most enjoyed eating— applesauce, cookies and cakes, pickles and jam. They all took prizes every year in the junior domestic arts section of the Prevost Valley Exhibition, partly because Mom (probably the most competitive person in the family) kept track of their creations, filled in the forms, paid the entrance fees, and got their entries out to the fairgrounds on time.

The summer Alex was thirteen, he baked a perfectly beautiful zucchini loaf that won not only a first prize ribbon, but the Domestic Arts Junior Championship rosette as well. He was pleased. The rosette lived on his bedroom wall for a long time, collecting dust. But he gave equal space and more importance to the awards he had earned for service.

Material success had never been a goal for Peter and me. That was certainly an area where our values matched those of the First Nations culture. When we met and married, Peter was in management at

Prevost Valley District Hospital; he was the assistant housekeeper. Zan and Tim were still under three when he switched to membership in the union, took a cut in pay, and became the hospital gardener. Gardeners, he determined, enjoyed more time at home, less stress at work, and weekends off. My nursing career had stopped years before, when we realized that our special needs children would require full-time parenting and we would have to raise our family on one income.

"It starts to feel better in here, more mellow," Peter whispered in my ear. Father Joe's homily was over—I had missed half of it—and now Rachael was getting ready to lead the next hymn.

"Jesus Loves Me," she announced. "It's not in the book; it's on your extra page." Protestant children going to Sunday School grew up with "Jesus Loves Me," but it wasn't familiar to most Roman Catholics. My kids had learned it at home, not at church. This had been Alex's favourite bedtime hymn.

Halfway through the first verse, the congregation started reaching for tissues and handkerchiefs. By the time we got to the first chorus there was an echoing chorus of noses being blown. Rachael had to hold it together by herself; very few people were able to sing. Even Clare's soaring soprano stalled. Was it the homily or the hymn, I wondered, that had set people off? Either way, Alex would have been delighted—all this emotion and all for him.

I felt obliged to join in the singing since the songs had been my choices. For the rest, I drifted through the service, noticing little beyond Tim's quiet tears, Alex's Godparents bringing the bread and wine up the aisle, and hugs from Peter and Mary Grace during the 'Peace.' Somebody seemed to be taking pictures—there was an occasional flash. And then Father Joe was saying the final prayers above Alex's casket and a nose-tickling smell of incense floated in the air.

As the pallbearers stepped into the aisle, ready to take Alex out to the waiting funeral coach, there was a slight kerfuffle in our row. Tim, who had been crying steadily for half an hour, suddenly found himself unable to face the big crowd sitting behind us. "I can't do it," he whispered desperately to Suzanne. Peter, realizing what was going on, quietly took Tim's place beside the casket.

Led by the cross bearer, and with Father Joe again bringing up the rear, Alex's procession moved slowly down the church. Each pallbearer held a casket handle, although, with the trolley in service, no effort was required. Directed by an unctuous usher, Suzanne and I followed Father Joe and the rest of our family followed us.

As the casket was being positioned, ready for its last lift into the funeral coach, a heavy set First Nations fellow elbowed Peter out of the way and relieved him of his burden. Seeing this, Zan refused to relinquish his handle until Alex's casket slid into the latch. Stanley closed the single padded door with a sigh of relief, and crisp white curtains hanging across the inside of the coach window swung back into place.

The Reception

A large First Nations assembly was standing outside in the damp parking lot. Many were Residential School survivors and their supporters, people who now refused to darken the doors of a Roman Catholic Church. They had been waiting patiently in the rain for well over an hour until Alex's funeral service was finished and his burial, the part that interested them, could finally get started. The First Nations people who had been inside now joined this crowd.

As the church emptied, the rest of the congregation split into several groups. Some, including Peter, went downstairs for coffee and sandwiches. Others, including Mary Grace and Sherry, got into their vehicles and drove out to St. Paul's graveyard. A few, including Clare and me, stayed by the church doors, waiting to see Alex being driven away. The First Nations crowd didn't move and neither did the funeral coach.

I turned to Clare and asked, almost frantically, "Why aren't they going? Why don't they just *go*?"

"They are waiting for you to leave, I think. Maybe it's another cultural thing." Clare put her arm around my shoulders and guided me toward the basement stairs. "Come on. Let's go down."

I glanced back from the top step. As the hearse still hadn't moved, Clare was probably right. I hadn't realized until now, but seeing Alex off for the last time had been particularly important to me. The consequent disappointment, a suddenly returning emotion

I had no trouble recognizing because Mary Grace and I had worked on it together, could be suppressed thanks to a few seconds of peace in the stairwell. I was glad Clare was with me. She waited while I unlocked the janitor's supply room and retrieved Alex's 'Life Story.' Alex's Godmother, Patricia, had promised to hand it out.

Opening the door to the main hall, we were met by a blast of noise. The bad acoustics meant that folks had to almost shout to be heard. Ever the janitor, my eyes went first to the floor. It was clean, with a nice deep shine and no scratches.

St. Cecelia's badly designed hall was functional, rather than comfortable, but Anita and her hard-working Compassion Committee always did their best to make the place look welcoming. For Alex's reception, small tables were covered with white, lace trimmed cloths. A bowl of flowers on each table was encircled with colourful handmade paper butterflies. Someone had brought the vases of purple lilac downstairs. Placed on a tall, double stand between two fire doors, the blossoms added a touch of elegance to the whole room.

At the back of the hall, a long table held platters of sandwiches, vegetable trays with dip, little squares of cheese, and bowls of pickles. People were already lined up, filling their plates. Cookies, squares, and cupcakes were set out on another long table on the far side. Closest to us there were drinks: coffee, tea, water, juice. I headed straight for the coffee queue, but Clare, right behind me, wisely advised tea.

Patricia came over, removed the pile of papers from my hand, and began distributing Alex's 'Life Story.' Most people did a quick skim and put it away to read later. Peter was across the hall talking to a group I didn't know—probably coworkers from the hospital. Clare suggested we get a sandwich and find a table, but I knew that both sitting down and eating were going to be impossible for me. The cup of tea was already a burden.

I wandered around the room, listening to anybody who wanted to talk and pausing for a moment here and there to answer questions but hardly concentrating. My thoughts were at Alex's graveside, not at his funeral reception. The tea, untasted, got left behind at every stop. Clare was vigilant; she retrieved my cup at intervals and brought it along behind me.

Most of the young people had gone to the graveyard but when the first half of the reception was nearly over and the early comers were beginning to leave, a girl approached me saying, "Hi, Mrs. Spencer."

I said a polite, "Hello," while doing my usual fast mental inventory. Was this a friend of a) James b) Zan c) Tim or d) Alex? Was she a) an old flame from years past, able to forgive my bad memory or b) someone more recent who might be easily insulted if unrecognized? Had she joined us for a) one of the important festivals like St. Nicholaas or Christmas or b) an ordinary family meal or c) a pit stop? Then I recognized a tattoo, and she slipped into place—this was Nettie, one of Tim's ex girlfriends. The two of them, along with Nettie's little son, had shared a disastrous move to Quebec three years ago. Zan had rescued Tim. Later on, Nettie had also come back to BC; this was my first reconnection with her.

"I hope you don't mind that I came," she said.

"Of course not!" I assured her. "It's nice to see you again. How is Braden? He must be almost ready for school."

"He's in kindergarten," said Nettie, pleased that I had remembered. "And doing very well," she added proudly. "But I'm sorry about Alex and Tim will sure miss him. He was a fun guy."

"Yes, he was," I agreed, although 'fun' wouldn't have been my adjective of choice.

"I was surprised to see such a large turnout of native people at the funeral. Alex used to stay away from them."

"He'd been a bit more involved with his birth family, the last few years," I said.

"It sure is a big family," Nettie observed. "Well, I'd better go before Tim and Suzanne get here. It was nice meeting you again." She slipped away into the crowd.

The people who had carpooled out to the graveyard were starting to arrive back at the church in twos and threes. Most, needing to warm up, headed straight for the tea and coffee.

"It was cold out there and they got Alex's name wrong," said Zan as he zipped past me, but Suzanne and Tim, who had travelled with him, stopped to talk. Suzanne was again unsettled. "They were collecting money," she said. "In *baskets*. In a *graveyard!*"

Tim added, "At first I figured the money was to pay for the food after the funeral, but then some people asked Frankie to go shopping in the mall because he was Alex's best friend. He's there now. They gave him all that money—he's supposed to buy some clothes and furniture and other stuff for Alex. I don't get it."

"It's for the Burning," I said. "Don't you remember? The Family wanted us to give them some of Alex's old clothes."

Tim was horrified. "They're going to burn brand new stuff? Why didn't they ask us for some of Alex's real furniture? His couch and bed are old and rickety."

"It's another cultural thing; they probably have their reasons," I said.

"Something else at the graveyard was 'cultural', and it worked out good," grinned Tim. "They had a shovel and they passed it around the circle —"

"Only to the men," Suzanne put in.

"— And the men were supposed to put a scoop of dirt on top of Alex. But they only gave the shovel to Indians. And they skipped Zan and me because we're the brothers. But then Steve reached out and grabbed it and when he was done he gave it to another white guy. Then it was for *all* the men." I could see that Tim had found this change of protocol very satisfying.

"They passed around a bowl of water, too," he added. "You were meant to wash your face in it and leave all your sorrow and tears at the graveyard. But I saw some eyelashes floating."

"You and Peter weren't the only ones they didn't want," said Suzanne. "Alex's friend, Kathy, got sent out of the graveyard because she's pregnant."

"Why?" I asked, but the kids didn't know.

Zan came back with coffee for himself and Suzanne. "Sorry, you have to get your own," he told Tim. "I only have two hands. Did you guys tell Mom about Alex's cross?"

"Not yet."

"The Family brought it," said Zan. "It's big! Varnished wood, handmade; I liked it a lot!" Zan loved working with wood. "And there's an eagle painted on the front. But the name is wrong. They put 'Alexander Bellman Jack.'"

"They couldn't allow him to be adopted," I sighed. "Or maybe it was started before they knew about his adoption. You guys had better get something to eat—this is lunch, don't forget."

"Just a moment, you haven't given me a hug." It was Sister Marianna, a longtime family friend who was popular with our adult children. Marianna lived in Victoria but her work often took her to the mainland. We had all been pleased that she was on the Island this week and could squeeze Alex's funeral into her busy schedule.

"The whole graveside service was nicely done, Ruth," she told me as the kids moved off toward the food tables. "Traditional but very low key. Mabel Jim was in charge. Do you know Mabel?"

I nodded. Everybody knew Mabel. She was a lay minister at St. Paul's and a Tzouhalem elder. Actually, she was an elder for all of us, not only the First Nations people. She had the love and esteem of all who knew her.

"Well, I have to tell you this before I get a sandwich," said Marianna. "The grave was ready, and we all gathered around it, and at that point, Alex's family of origin tried to take over. They weren't rude or anything but they wanted things to be done the Tzou'in'quam way. Mabel said, in her soft voice, 'This is Tzouhalem land, and we will be having a Tzouhalem ceremony.' And that's exactly what we had. It was lovely."

She looked across at Tim, who was busy piling a plate high with cheese and pickles. "Tim was very distressed out at the graveyard," she said, "but I think he's doing better now."

Sister Marianna moved on, and Clare came back to me with the inevitable cup of tea. "It's fresh," she said, "and I'm going to stay right here until you drink it."

"Good for you, Clare." Mary Grace had returned with Sherry. "Hi, Ruth," she said. "Don't talk; get that down."

Feeling ready for something hot and wet, and thankful for a firm directive, I gratefully took the cup from Clare and wrapped both hands around its comforting warmth. Mary Grace, working against the echoing hall, almost shouted introductions —"Sherry, this is Ruth's friend, Clare. Clare, this is Sherry, Alex's coroner." I sipped the hot tea and looked around the room.

Tim and Zan, sitting with Suzanne and some other young folks, had been well supplied—someone had brought a whole tray of sandwiches to their table. Peter was still surrounded by friends; I wondered if he had found time to eat. Bruce was back from taking our mother home and was busy filling two small plates with cookies and squares for himself and Allanah. Beside the door, a group of Alex's ex girlfriends huddled around a table with their heads close together. They needn't have worried about privacy because no one could hear them in the acoustical din that was St. Cecelia's basement.

I turned back to Sherry. "Could you finally send the police home?"

"We left one member out at St. Paul's," said Sherry. "He was going to stay until the excavator finished; he's probably gone by now."

"I was standing beside Sherry," Mary Grace told me. "Near the end of the service someone produced a shovel, and all the men took a turn putting soil on the casket. And with each shovelful, Sherry whispered to me, 'I think it's going to be okay. I think it's going to be okay.'"

Sherry smiled. "And I had to hold Mary Grace back," she said. "When she discovered the shovelling was only for the men, she wanted to take a stand for women's rights."

There was no longer a row of people in front of the tea and coffee. Clare herded us in that direction, found an empty table, and signalled to Peter, who came over holding a large platter of sandwiches and a small plate of sweets. While the four of them ate lunch, and I had another cup of tea, Mary Grace and Sherry shared their perceptions of the extremely crowded graveside service. Many of The Family hadn't gone to the church at all, not even to the parking lot, Sherry told us. They had been waiting at the graveyard.

"They covered Alex's casket with the most beautiful blanket," Mary Grace said. "I wish you could have seen it, Ruth."

"You will," said Tim, looming up behind Peter. "The lady who was taking pictures in church? That's our landlady. She had her camera at the graveyard, too, but the Indians don't allow that. They asked her to leave. She didn't listen, so one of the cops took her outside the gate."

"Well, it's fair that she got kicked out," I said, "but I sure hope I get to see her pictures."

"I'll work on it," Tim promised. "We're ready to go home. Do you think we would be allowed to take some sandwiches? There's lots left."

"Let's ask the committee." I led the way to the kitchen, where one of the ladies was already covering the leftovers with plastic wrap. Anita handed Tim a plate of sandwiches and another of mixed cookies.

"What about the rest of the food, Ruth?" she asked. "Should we send it all over to the food bank?"

"Heck, no," I said. "We've got half of the food bank's clients right here. Let them take all of it along when they go home—they'll be the last to leave—and that will save you or somebody else from making an extra trip downtown."

Tim went around the room spreading a "free food" message to all the people he recognized as food bank regulars, asking them to come to the kitchen when they were ready to leave. I suspected a party was being organized; Tim kept stopping here and there for a quiet little comment directly into somebody's ear. An especially long pause at the ex girlfriends' table confirmed my suspicions.

"The more they take, the better," I told Anita. "Some of them are planning an event for tonight—they'll all be together, somewhere, drowning their sorrows. Those sandwiches will help sop up the alcohol."

The hall was starting to empty. Peter stood up as I returned to our table; he was ready to go home. Clare, Sherry, and Mary Grace began retrieving their jackets and bags. Zan joined the general move toward the doors, collecting a covered plate of sandwiches on his way out.

"It's a good idea, Mom," he said when I offered a slight protest. "You won't have to make supper—we can finish these off."

"Um..." I agreed halfheartedly. "You know, I'm feeling very

guilty, leaving all this cleaning up for other people to do. Should we stay and help?"

"We're not staying," Peter said.

"This time, the other people are doing the work for you," said Mary Grace as we climbed the stairs. "And they want it that way."

Clare added, "Ruth, you always stay on until the last dog is hung. Give yourself a break."

The rain had stopped, but a chilly breeze swirled around us as we stepped outside. The sky was a dreary grey. The parking lot's bleak concrete surface was covered with ruffled puddles. Many of the cars had already disappeared. There was no funeral coach, no police vehicle, no silent crowd.

Rather than feeling released from anxiety and stress, I had a sudden sense of anticlimax. In an instant, trauma had shifted to dull routine. Alex was gone; our dramatic week was over; even the promise of an early summer had vanished. With a gloom matching the weather, I realized that my conveniently missing emotions were going to return as they had before, in unpredictable ways.

Mary Grace knew what I was thinking. Giving me a quick hug, she whispered, "Don't worry, let yourself be sad, and I'll see you on Thursday."

The Burning

Peter and I drove home silently; there seemed to be nothing left to say. Three dogs didn't even bother to bark, our house was empty and echoing, the phone had stopped ringing at last. I wished we had invited somebody talkative over for the rest of the day to relieve this terrible silence. Zan planned to stay for the night and was driving up the hills behind us—he had remembered, at the last moment, to go back for Alex's flowers—but Zan wasn't one to chatter.

The rest of the afternoon dragged. Zan read a book. Peter got caught up on a week's worth of newspapers. I washed a few dishes in the kitchen and had started an aimless tidying of my office when a group of short ideas slid into my mind. With luck on my side, and with catching the moment, these clusters of phrases often became a poem. I enjoyed that kind of writing but didn't always have access to it. My short ideas were mostly a product of suppressed emotions. Grabbing a pencil and paper—no time now to wait for the computer to warm up—I dropped into my office chair and started to write.

> Centre of the church and centre of attention
> — the casket; long and grey and cold,
> covered with an off white pall
> draped by his aunt and teacher.
> Their last official duty.

> Rows and rows of mourners,
> clean cut and conservative.
> Relatives, associates,
> companions of a lifetime,
> my supporters during crises.
>
> And many vacuous young adults,
> low cut, bare bellied, pierced, tattooed,
> the marginalized, the ostracized,
> riffraff of our community,
> the local food bank regulars.
>
> My friends …and his.
>
> He would have loved this funeral;
> the feuding of two families,
> the stress of the arrangements,
> the lilac and the music,
> the admiring eulogy
> and himself, star of the show.
> Too bad he had to miss it.
>
> Did you think, because I could still laugh,
> I didn't care?
> You said, "You never cried."
> Of course there were no tears;
> my grieving has been going on for years.

This poem, with its sharp memories and soothing last lines, came together without difficulty. By the time the first draft was finished, and the penciled original had been put into my poetry file, it was long past our usual suppertime.

We were beginning to eye Zan's platter of sandwiches with faint interest when the dogs left their mats in front of the fire and pushed their way to the door, barking excitedly.

Looking out the window, Zan said, "There's a rusty old jalopy coming down the driveway."

"Oh, no," I protested. "Not again."

"I gather you know who it is," observed Zan.

"Richard Wilson," I groaned. "Why on earth is he here?"

"More trouble," said Peter grimly, as he went to the door.

The dogs rushed outside to sniff around the strange car, ignoring Richard. Peter, stiffly polite, invited him to come in. He walked through to the living room amidst a hostile atmosphere where Zan's was the only friendly face.

But even before he spoke we could sense in Richard a dignity and a quiet self-assurance that had been missing the day before. This was, Peter and I quickly realized, a different personality. Yesterday we had coped with a boy—today we were encountering a man.

Zan walked over, shook hands, and introduced himself. Peter asked Richard to sit down. I said nothing; I wasn't prepared to be gracious to any member of The Family.

Richard looked directly at me. "You probably don't want me here," he said gravely, "and I can't blame you for that. But coming to talk to you guys is part of my job."

Zan said, "Mom told me your family is traditionally responsible for all the Tzouhalem burials."

"Yes, organizing the burials and the Burnings, too," Richard confirmed. "Part of our responsibility is to get the word out and to be sure everybody knows what's going on. That's why I came—to tell you about the Burning we just had for Alex."

I said, "Actually, I'm not interested." Peter gave me a surprised look; he wasn't used to hearing me express myself in such definite terms. But I had been doing some research. After Stanley asked us to bring in Alex's old clothes for the Burning, I had turned to the internet for an explanation of this Coast Salish tradition. The First Nations people believe in the continuity of life between this world and the spirit world. They believe their dead live on in the spirit world and can communicate with them through community rituals.

And so a Burning was a social custom used to send food, clothing, and personal belongings, everything that would be needed in the spirit world, to the person who had died. The act of burning permitted these effects to move from the physical to the spiritual. As the smoke went up, its sacred component went on to the spirit world and the dead received the essence of the food and possessions they had been used to. For the living, this was a way to show respect and to continue the care of their loved ones. And, through the smoke of a ritual Burning, the person who had died was able to communicate directly with those who were still alive.

Apart from my belief in the continuity of life between this world and the spirit world, all that I knew about a Burning went against my personal values. I didn't want anything to do with it.

"Well, I would like to hear about it," Zan remarked pointedly.

Richard continued to address me. "This is important, Ruth." Instinctively choosing the right bait he added, "The elders asked me to come."

That made all the difference. There would have been many elders present at this Burning, but the two who understood and accepted me, Alex's birth grandmother and his Aunty Loretta, had my admiration and respect.

"I'll listen," I murmured.

"Good," said Richard. "Alex spoke to us through the elders, and he had a lot to say. And he told us he wanted to be called 'Alex,' not 'Bellman.'"

Richard sat straight in his chair, his whole attitude one of calm attentiveness. It was almost as if he had wrapped a garment of formality about himself before he started to speak.

"The first thing Alex said was 'This is Alex. I have crossed the river and the elders are taking care of me.'"

I immediately acknowledged the integrity of the elder who had received and shared this message. Alex's greatest need, always, was to be cared for. Ever since childhood, he had required more support and security than his siblings seemed to need. It made perfect sense to me that this would be part of his first statement.

Alex's words were being received by aboriginal people and of course they would be couched in the terminology his listeners understood. But the ancestors Alex would have recognized were the deceased members of his adoptive family who had shared their love with him long before he entered the spirit world. His Oma, Peter's mother, would be there, and the great aunts and uncles he remembered. His two grandfathers, my dad and Peter's, who both died long before Alex was born, were familiar to him through photos, his parents' memories, and their often told stories.

There was even a little joke in Alex's first remark. When he was old enough to answer the phone he had been taught to say, "Hello, this is Alex." But he had slurred it into "Thi Salex" causing his older brothers to tease him. He had quickly switched to, "Alex speaking."

Richard went on. "'Please tell my mother and father, Peter and Ruth, I am happy and safe,'" he said, then, "'Please tell my mom and dad, Peter and Ruth, I love them.'"

Again, I was impressed by the honesty and openness of the elders delivering Alex's messages. They had been involved in the last five days of family trauma. It would have been easy for them to withhold the "Peter and Ruth."

Richard must have guessed my thoughts. "Alex sure let us know who his mom and dad were," he said ruefully. "Almost all his words, even the ones for other people, had 'Peter and Ruth' in there someplace. And he said, 'Please tell Peter and Ruth that I love them,' about five times."

There were a few more general comments intended for everybody, followed by another one for us: "'Tell my mother and father, Peter and Ruth, I have been walking in the gardens beside the river. It is very beautiful here.'"

"That's about it," said Richard, "except for something kind of strange."

Through the elders, Alex had thanked his First Nations community for the things they had sent him, particularly the clothes, the books and magazines, and his desk. Richard knew all those things had been burned; he had put them on the fire himself. But then Alex had said, "Thanks for the music." Richard was positive no radios, records, soundtracks, or cassettes had gone up in the smoke." I don't know where that came from," he said.

All of a sudden I remembered the unsuccessful searching Cricket, Tim and I had done for a particular Guns N' Roses album. Alex was thanking the three of us for our intentions and efforts, even though, in the end, his favourite cassette hadn't been played at his funeral. This was a special little remark for the three of us, something nobody at the Burning could have known or guessed.

It was quiet in our living room. The sharply edged lack of noise we had struggled against ever since we came home from Alex's funeral was gone. In its place, there was a soft silence of tranquility and peace. For the first time in days, I heard Peter's big clock ticking.

Richard had said everything he came to say. He stood up, ready to go. Zan and Peter shook his hand. I crossed the living room and gave him a hug. Still without speaking, we followed him out the door and paused in wonder at the top of the steps.

The clouds had gone. The sky was clear. In the west, a flaming sun slid down behind our tall, black fir trees, spreading brilliant orange banners far across the sky. Orange—Alex's favourite colour. As Richard's old car rattled its way up the driveway and out onto the road, we watched the glowing sky fade to peach and pale into night.

Appendix i

Elaine and James were asleep when the phone rang, just before 7a.m., on that fateful Thursday morning. James answered, still half asleep.

While he asked short, sharp questions: "Is Dad okay?" "What happened?" "How did you find out?"— and listened to long answers, Elaine tried to guess what the conversation was about, but for once she couldn't read James's emotions. When James had finished, and silently stretched across to put the phone away, Elaine asked, "Well? Are you going to tell me what's going on?"

"It's horrible news."

"Are you going to tell me anyway?"

"Alex died. It was a suicide."

"*What*?"

"It was a suicide."

Elaine fell back on the bed, totally shocked.

She found herself remembering the Mother's Day picnic, three evenings before. Alex had seemed a bit frustrated with the pressure he was getting from his birth family to move to the reserve. He had told Elaine, "They have too many expectations," and had added with his quirky grin, "You'll have to kidnap me out of Alderlea." Elaine had laughed, "Well, sure! We'll do that as soon as we get back from Hawaii."

Elaine knew about the series of emails being exchanged, through

Mom, between Alex and Cricket. Alex's birth family wanted him to organize a transfer of little Kaitlyn's health insurance. During the picnic, Mom said to Alex, "I had another email from Cricket. She said don't do anything about Kaitlyn's medical coverage. She's got everything she needs under the Alberta system. I'll give you a copy of the letter before you go home."

Alex wasn't particularly pleased with this. He didn't care about shifting Kaitlyn over to Band coverage; that was something the birth family thought important. What he wanted, he told Elaine, was some contact with Cricket. But Cricket didn't want any interference from Alex when things were finally regrouped for Kaitlyn, and she didn't want anybody from Tzou'in'quam Band to have her address, her email, or her phone number.

Elaine and James drove Alex home after Dad's birthday party on the following Tuesday evening, with a stop for gasoline on the way. Using his status card, Alex could get tax-free gas for others, and he often supported his brothers in this way. Alex asked them to come up for a last cup of coffee, but they wanted to get back home before dark.

When she first heard the dreadful news on Thursday morning, Elaine was afraid Alex had committed suicide right after they had dropped him at his door. She said she was thankful to realize Alex's death had occurred about twenty four hours after she had last seen him.

Following Mom's phone call about Alex, Elaine expected James to fall apart immediately, but it was a while before he started crying. As for Elaine herself, she felt she had to stay strong for James, and they were in their hotel room in Hawaii before she finally let go. By then they were able to comfort each other, and Elaine encouraged James to share some stories about when he and Alex were children. The first thing James remembered—of course—was the farting contests he and Alex used to have when they were supposed to be sleeping.

A few days later they went shopping, looking for Hawaiian souvenirs to take back to Canada for their families. When James said, "And something for Alex," Elaine thought he was in denial, but James said he had been thinking about this, and he wanted to get some nice artificial leis for Alex's graveside service. He cried a bit in the store.

Elaine said she was aware of James' grief all through their holiday, particularly when he struggled with seasickness during the last two days of their cruise. By the time they got home she wasn't in very good shape herself. James mixed each of them a Happy Homecoming drink, and he made hers too strong; she was crying and sick all night. The next day, she was too sick to visit Alex's grave. James went with Tim, instead.

For Elaine, any phone calls really early in the morning are still scary. All her friends know to call after 8:30 a.m.

By Elaine and Ruth

Appendix ii

The Quarry

…He waved…
They laughed and signalled back.
…He smiled and called…
They yelled, "Come out! It's time to go!"
…and then he turned a bluish grey,
spiralling slowly downwards through the water…
Many lithe young bodies dived to save him
much too late.
The quarry had just claimed another victim.

Someone had a cell phone (unusual in those days)
and called for help through 911.
The families with children stopped collecting their belongings.
The groups of teens with attitude put away their alcohol.
Somebody ran up the road to move a car
and clear the barrier marked 'Stay Out.'
'This is Private Property.' 'No Access in Emergencies.'
Rescue crews lost precious moments
trying to unlock the gate

and silence echoed round the quarry
as they brought the body up.

While the people at the quarry
waited grimly for a rescue that wasn't going to happen,
neighbourhoods were rallying.
A meeting place was organized
—a hall where families could collect;
support for all the witnesses; coffee, juice, and sandwiches;
grief counselling laid on in bulk.

My two braindamaged adult sons were present at the drowning.
That afternoon, a group of friends decided to go swimming;
the driver of their carload was the fellow who had died.
One son knew him only from two barhopping evenings.
The other son could claim a slight acquaintance;
for a week they'd shared a kitchen in someone else's house.
But now that he was suddenly terribly important
he was more than just their driver.
He'd become "Our Closest Friend."

One son had audacity. The other had a license
and a streetwise little girlfriend with an innocent expression,
who told police, through pouring tears,
"We all came out together" and
"Our things are in that yellow car. Can't we go home?"
They drove over to the hall for free sandwiches and coffee,
but they definitely didn't want a soothing of excitement.
To de-escalate was boring; they wanted stimulation
so they went up to Emergency hoping for some action.
Then they had to find a party to show off their new wheels;
a fun trip to Victoria was indicated.
Three days later, at the funeral, they finally returned the car.

My younger son, FASD, and always very self-absorbed,
became quite sorry for himself as life got back to normal.

Identifying with his friend
soon had my son believing that he had "caused the accident."
Left to himself, he'd find a way to get out to the quarry
and sit brooding on the bank in morbid melancholy,
waiting to be noticed.

Luckily, this is the son who gets despondent publicly.
Keeping feelings private is a skill that still escapes him.
His anxiety neurosis keeps enthusiasm high
regarding visits to his doctors,
and he values medications. Prescriptions prove he's really sick.
Some maternal interference
with fast tracking of appointments and suggestions to his doctor
clarified the situation.
And my life returned to 'normal'
as concentration on his health
made my son forget about the quarry.

Ruth (1999)

Appendix iii

WE REMEMBER[5]

Alexander Bellman Spencer
Born October 20, 1976
Died May 20, 2002 at age 25

By Ruth Spencer, Alex's mother

When Alex died, a magazine that had already published three of his pieces was asking to see more of his work. People who had heard him speak at workshops said they couldn't believe how much they had learned. The many young women present at his funeral told me about seeing him on television: "He was so cute!" My son was not an actor, not a polished writer, not an exceptional public speaker, but he was a skillful communicator and an expert on his own subject, the invisible disabilities and complications of living with a Fetal Alcohol Spectrum Disorder.

Alex was born with Fetal Alcohol Syndrome. When he joined our family he was small for his age, had not yet attempted to walk or talk, and saw himself as 'little and cute.' With two other boys in

---

5   First published by SNAP Newsmagazine Volume 19 Number 2

his age group—all three under three—we were a good fit for Alex. Physically, he caught up quickly; emotionally, he was often ahead of the pack. But as he grew older, we knew there were going to be challenges.

"He can't keep track of his own belongings and he wears the first jacket he comes to," said his kindergarten teacher. "But he will always get by on his charm." In grade one, the teacher said, "Alex is happiest on days when our regular routine is closely followed. He doesn't handle change very well." In grade two, "Alex is still in the slow arithmetic group, but everyone wants to be his partner. He is friendly, outgoing, and popular." In grade three, "Alex tries hard. He is eager and enthusiastic, although his enthusiasm is not always well directed."

Nobody knew that Alex had permanent and irreversible brain damage or that he was already struggling with the severe deficits of an FASD. His learning skills and memory were intermittent. He was sometimes unable to differentiate between reality and fantasy. He couldn't make the connections between cause and effect. His impulse control was poor and his reasoning abilities were almost nonexistent. Unfortunately, because he was attractive, always smartly dressed, and had developed excellent verbal skills, he appeared to be far more capable than he actually was. By the time Alex entered middle school his teachers were saying, "He must be more responsible," and "He must try harder." They didn't understand that he was unable, not unwilling.

As Alex grew older other health issues surfaced. Our family doctor organized a referral to Sunny Hill Hospital in Vancouver where he tested positive for Fetal Alcohol Syndrome. But having a diagnosis turned out to be a hollow victory. There were no services, anywhere, for people with an FASD, and no one, apart from family, was the least bit interested. Alex's invisible disabilities, although they affected every part of his life, remained generally unacknowledged until, as an adult, he became part of Finding Alternative Solutions.

When Alex died, the coroner said, "Alex did not intend to end his life. He died because of his poor balance, and, as his doctor said, 'because he was playing a dangerous game.' This was the closest thing to an accident that a suicide could ever be."

Alex didn't die because he was suicidal or depressed. He died because he had a Fetal Alcohol Spectrum Disorder.

About the Author

Three adopted children with Fetal Alcohol Spectrum Disorder plus forty-eight years as a parent advocate have made Ruth Spencer an authority on the subject of FASD behaviours, even though she describes herself as "An ordinary mom with no letters after my name."

In 1994, at the request of other parents in her FASD support group, Ruth started to write about the challenges involved in loving, accepting, and supporting her older teenagers with FASD. There were long hours in Youth Court, where, "Everybody but me understood the system." There were visits to jails: "Once I was locked into the washroom by a guard with a real gun in his belt." There were many trips to Emergency, a crisis pregnancy, evictions, street living, sexually transmitted diseases, overdose, welfare fraud, alcohol abuse, and psych ward stays. Ruth never ran short of new material. By 1998, her articles and poems were being published in Canadian magazines.

"The Burning: Parenting my son through adoption, FASD, and suicide," is her first full-length book. It covers events following the accidental suicide of her youngest son, born with Fetal Alcohol Syndrome. "The writing was hard and intense; it took a long time. But I had to write this book for the sake of other adoptive parents who are navigating adoption reunions with their FASD affected children."

Now a grandmother, Ruth is still parenting her adult children with FASD.

Book Club Questions

1. The World Health Organization has officially recognized Fetal Alcohol Spectrum Disorder as a global problem. In Canada there are more than one million people with an FASD. Do you know anybody living with this condition?
2. Has this book increased your knowledge and understanding of the difficulties people with an FASD must surmount every day?
3. Do you believe FASD is totally preventable? Why? …or why not?
4. Would you be willing to adopt or be a grandparent to a child who might have an FASD?…or a child who has already been diagnosed with Fetal Alcohol Syndrome?
5. In Canada there are more than 10 suicides daily. Has suicide touched your family? Did you get the support you needed? How can hope and resilience be offered to potential suicide victims??
6. The Burning deals with cultural differences. How controversial are the issues raised?
7. Was there something surprising or unusual in this story?
8. How did this book challenge or change your views?
9. What feedback would you give the author?

Who owns the body?

Peter and Ruth Spencer have received impossible news – the suicide of Alex, their youngest son. They are the parents of five adult children; James and Zan who are genetically linked; Kathleen, Tim, and Alex who are adopted. Now Alex's family of origin, believing the adoption was never finalized, wants his body.

The Family first threatens to steal Alex's body and then, at a series of Big House meetings, plans to get a court injunction. They want to put the funeral and burial on hold and the body on ice until Alex is legally their property. Alex's parents must put aside their grieving as they search for proof of their son's adoption and wait to hear if they will be allowed to take care of his final arrangements.

A Salish First Nations cultural event, a Burning, helps both families come to terms with their loss.